GIRLS' PUBLIC DAY SCHOOL TRUST

T0381614

PLATE I

Mrs WILLIAM GREY

The JUBILEE BOOK *of the*
Girls' Public Day School Trust
1873–1923

by

LAURIE MAGNUS, M.A.
Vice-Chairman of the Council

CAMBRIDGE
AT THE UNIVERSITY PRESS
1923

CAMBRIDGE
UNIVERSITY PRESS

University Printing House, Cambridge CB2 8BS, United Kingdom

Published in the United States of America by Cambridge University Press, New York

Cambridge University Press is part of the University of Cambridge.

It furthers the University's mission by disseminating knowledge in the pursuit of education, learning and research at the highest international levels of excellence.

www.cambridge.org
Information on this title: www.cambridge.org/9781107685574

© Cambridge University Press 1923

First published 1923
First paperback edition 2014

A catalogue record for this publication is available from the British Library

ISBN 978-1-107-68557-4 Paperback

PREFACE

THIS BOOK is the outcome of the wish of the Council of the Girls' Public Day School Trust to commemorate in written form the jubilee of its foundation. The occasion was commemorated orally by a solemn Service of Thanksgiving, celebrated, by permission, in St Paul's Cathedral, on Friday, June 1st, 1923, when the memorial sermon was preached by the Very Rev. Dr Inge, Dean of St Paul's.

Our jubilee is a movable feast. The Memorandum and Articles of Association of the Girls' Public Day School Company (later, the Trust) were registered on June 19th, 1872; our last School, at Birkenhead, was opened on September 24th, 1901. Each of our Schools keeps its own anniversaries, but since the active work of the Trust started in 1873, when its two first Schools were opened, the present year is, properly, its jubilee.

I did not know, when I undertook to write the book, how heavy the task would prove. Still less did I know how amply I should be assisted, nor how inadequately I should rise to the hopes of my assistants. When I add that my two chief coadjutors have been two past Head-mistresses of Trust Schools, Mrs Woodhouse and Miss Hastings, whose names and acts are recorded in Chapter IV, it will be seen that a high standard was set to me. Mrs Woodhouse, a member of our Council, entered the service of the Trust in 1878, and Miss Hastings, a member of our Education Committee, in 1876. Thus, their co-operation dates back almost to the beginning of our existence, and the chronicler in 1923 has enjoyed the unique advantage of drawing on their memory as well as on their stored enthusiasm. Another valuable coadjutor has been my colleague, Mr G. H.

Hallam, who contributed several sections to Chapter IV; and the proofs of the whole book have been read, to its great advantage, by the Chairman of Council, Mr Llewelyn Davies, by the Hon. Lady Digby, Vice-President, and by the Secretary, Mr Maclean. They have saved me from many mistakes, and made many useful suggestions. In what is lacking still, I am to blame.

I have not used all the material with which I have been so generously supplied. It was difficult to draw the line between a book replete with details relating only to our Schools and a book which might possess some interest in the history of education in the nineteenth century. Thus, I have not included lists of names of holders of scholarships, prize-winners, and so forth. Nor have I referred, except in passing, to the work of the Schools in war-time. It was a wonderfully creditable record, kept up with undiminished vigour till the end, but, after all, everybody was doing it. More doubtful, perhaps, is the decision to omit specialist contributions on such topics as Music, Drawing, Physical Training, Games, Training for Teaching, the Junior School, etc. They seemed to me to lie a little outside the scope of a jubilee volume, and my colleagues have been good enough to leave me discretion in the matter.

But a few words on some of those topics may, perhaps, be added here. Thus, Kensington, pre-eminently, and Streatham Hill are among the Schools with a special interest in music, and reference may be made to the article on "Music" by Miss Ethel Home, Headmistress at Kensington, in the *Journal of Education*, October, 1922. A debt of gratitude is due to our Music Advisory Board, and particularly to the late Dr C. H. Lloyd and to Dr Ernest Walker. Drawing, again, has been included in our curricula since the earliest days, and we passed through various experiments till, in 1909,

an Art Advisory Board, consisting of Mr George
Clausen, R.A., Prof. Tonks, Mr Selwyn Image, Mr
Vignoles Fisher and Mr A. S. Hartrick, gave us the
benefit of their expert help. They inspect and examine
the Schools periodically, and have drawn up simple
canons of art-teaching for the use of the mistresses,
with the result that the Board of Education says:
"The Board feel no doubt that the influence of the Art
Advisory Board as at present exercised, with the annual
opportunity to review the work being done in the
Schools, helps to maintain interest and effort among
the teachers and to ensure a high standard of work. I
am to add that the Inspectors were greatly interested
in the exhibition of works. They were impressed by the
generally excellent quality of the teaching and the
knowledge and understanding of the purpose and
limitations of school work which were shown." A
tribute should be paid in this connection to the
splendid work of Miss Welch in the Clapham High
School Art Training Department.

We take, too, no little pride in the Training Departments of some of the larger Schools, where the main
principle was laid down by the late Miss Gavin, of
Wimbledon, in a paper read in 1906 before the Headmistresses' Association. A teacher's preparation, she
said, should "proceed more from the concrete to the
abstract," and "the theoretical work in such training
should be supplementary to the practical work."

Fuller extracts may be permitted from a memorandum
prepared for this volume on the Junior School, since its
place in secondary education has become, or is becom-
ing, a somewhat urgent question of administration and
finance. In this connection the following paragraphs
are of general interest:

"Provision is made in all our Schools for children from the

age of five, a separate house being taken for them in many instances. The parents' appreciation is shown by the fact that almost as many little boys as girls under the age of nine (after which boys are not usually admitted) are to be found in their preparatory classes.

In most Schools the conditions provided for the little ones are such as all lovers of children desire to secure for every child in the land—a garden, with trees, flowers and birds—bright, airy class-rooms—a large room where free movement is possible— classes small enough to allow of much individual guidance— skilled observation of health and development.

In the next stage of the Junior School which according as the little girl's progress fits her to go forward may be from the age of 7, 8 or 9 to 10, 11 or 12—the aim is the successful linking of the earlier stage with that where Secondary education begins. A broad base of interests, and the power of grasping new facts and new ideas intelligently, are the educational aims kept in view, rather than the attainment of a definite standard in particular subjects. It is well known that under the same conditions different children progress at very different rates in learning, e.g. to write correct English or to work Arithmetic; and that some who have much difficulty in one or other of these subjects may possess reasoning power or artistic gifts far above the average.

Many girls pass through their School from the lowest to the highest Form; they are found to be an element of stability and a channel of good tradition that are of the utmost value."

The Council would very much deplore any threat to the maintenance of these Departments.

I spoke above of the heaviness of this task, but I meant really the heaviness of the responsibility. It has been a labour of love to compile the book, and I can but hope that it is not quite unworthy of the noble lives which it commemorates.

L. M.

THE ATHENÆUM,
PALL MALL, S.W. 1,
June, 1923.

CONTENTS

PLATES

THANKSGIVING

Though ye have passed, our Ladies of the Schools,
Who laid the stones, and set the temperate rules,
    And broke untrodden paths with Spring reveal'd,

We do not pass, who, in a later day,
Your chosen message with new valiance say,—
    "Knowledge is now no more a fountain seal'd."

Behold, our gardens flourish with your flowers,
Sown in a time austerer far than ours,
    But, ah! how much less frugal in design.

We have outgrown the halls ye wrought to build,
But the large hopes that haunt them, unfulfill'd,
    No perishable tenements confine.

There climb our thoughts to meet you, our thanks climb.
We seek you on the tranquil heights of time,
    Bringing one garland from our fifty years.

Take it, this pious tribute of our love,
This emblem of the plan ye guard above,
    This human utterance framed for sainted ears.

CHAPTER I

THE DAUGHTERS' NEED

NO account of girls' education, however limited its scope, can neglect the fifth chapter of *Education in the Nineteenth Century*, edited by Dr R. D. Roberts for the publishers of the present volume. The papers contained in that history were read in August, 1900, at the Summer Meeting of the Cambridge University Extension Society, and Miss F. Gadesden, Headmistress of our Blackheath School from 1886 till 1919, contributed the lecture on "The Education of Girls." She was fortunate in finding ready to hand, in a recent issue of the *Modern Language Quarterly*, the authentic diary of a schoolgirl, who had been at school in Yorkshire under the redoubtable Miss Richmal Mangnall (1769–1820), and the contrast between Miss Mangnall and Miss Gadesden, as heads of girls' schools, is hardly less striking in real life than that between the boys' headmasters in *Nicholas Nickleby* and *Tom Brown's Schooldays*. This diary, which was kept by Elizabeth Firth, later a friend of the Brontë family, and godmother to Anne and Emily, is delicious in its inclusions and omissions. "Our class of geography were two hours looking for the Emperor of Persia's name. My governess told us it was Mahomet," runs one of the entries. But if they were weak on the names of Persian Emperors, "I got the names of the Kings of England," runs another, and "began of reading ancient history," runs a third. A "brain-day" was the description of a day when a *viva voce* examination was held, no doubt on the lines of the famous *Questions*: "We had a brain-day in Geography; I had seven mistakes, which was the least of any one." (Perhaps she had remembered that Mahomet was King of Persia.) But Miss Firth was as good at deportment as at geography: "Miss Fayrer gave 270 words of dictionary for poking; I had ten." The punishment seldom fitted the crime: "Miss Ropers were sent to Coventry till they would say their Catechism. Some of the ladies"—they were never girls— "had the Epistle and Gospels, twenty-eight verses, for writing on their desks." And there was a lot of "whiping" (with one *p*), though it did not teach Miss Firth how to spell "ippertinance."

"Of the moral tone among the 'ladies'," writes Miss Gadesden, "and the absence of training in honour and unselfishness and public spirit the diary is significant.... Brilliant exceptions there doubtless were, but is it any wonder that the majority of girls brought up in such a moral atmosphere should have gone back to their homes selfish, prejudiced and helpless, with no object beyond their own pleasures, and no appreciation or understanding of their duties, and of obligations to themselves and others? This is a type of a school which provided for the rich daughters of England. For the poorer there was no provision at all."

How the few "brilliant exceptions" attempted in the next generation to change the rule for "the majority of girls"; how their work was spread in extension to the "poorer" more directly than to the rich, and in intension to departments of life which had suggested no questions to Miss Mangnall; how the "ladies" were turned back to girls, and were then turned into public schoolgirls; and how Miss Mangnall herself, with her catechism and birch-rod, was replaced by the great and gracious teachers whose acquaintance it will be our privilege to make: this, briefly, is the subject of our jubilee memoir of the Girls' Public Day School Trust, founded in time in 1872, but founded securely in spirit on women's capacity and worth.

The perception that *better* schools were wanted was a matter of slow growth, all the slower, no doubt, because of the existence of the worse schools. Mr Sidney Webb has somewhere pointed out that England, unlike some other countries, has derived its education in the main from a species of philanthropy. The ragged-school was the father of the Board School. Little English children were first taught the rudiments of humane learning, by Act of Parliament and at the public expense, not because learning was desirable, nor because Pierian pioneers had discovered that "knowledge is now no more a fountain sealed" (the motto selected for the schools of the Girls' Public Day School Company), but because compulsory schooling seemed, on the whole, the best way of rescuing the children from the gutter. State education, historically, was not an end in itself, but a means to social reform. It was an experiment in philanthropy, not culture, and lawyers still refer to the still famous case of Regina *v.* Cockerton in order to prove that public money voted for purposes of education is intended rather to save children from worse than to prepare them for better things.

Our girls' public schools, on the contrary, owed their rise to no other cause than the need of better schools for girls. And the need of them had to be proved— always a difficult matter—in the face of vested interests in existing schools. Even if they had not arisen, or had not arisen at that time, not one little middle-class girl would therefore have been educationally derelict. The only result would have been that another generation of partially incomplete English womanhood would have grown to maturity in the era of light and expansion in which the nineteenth century closed. No: the children who entered our schools were not in danger of any actual harm; they were only missing a potential good. They were receiving a kind of education—enough to shelter them from evil, and to persuade them to stay within their shelter; they were not receiving the kind of education best suited to their capacities and powers. The pious founders of the High Schools, unlike the early State educators, were not planting in the desert. They had to pull down before they could build up. They had to substitute efficiency, system, scholarship, regular hours, a logical curriculum, and careful team-work, for the unmethodized habits of an untrained governess in the schoolroom. All honour, then, to the pioneers, and, particularly, to the pioneers from the schoolroom— Miss Pipe of Laleham, Miss Lowman of Chelsea, Miss Buss and Miss Beale; the Governesses' Benevolent Institution and the London Association of Schoolmistresses,—who laboured on in those early days, and who were fighting ideas as well as words. For behind their resolve to convert the "young ladies'" "select establishments" into girls' schools *tout court*, lay the resolve to reform the methods and to evoke recognition for their own ideals.

Evidence to the strength of the daughters' need may be sought from many sources: most scientifically, perhaps, from the *Report* of the Royal Commission on the Education of Girls, which was appointed in 1867, or from the Appendix (of horrible examples) to a paper on the Education of Women, read, in connection with that *Report*, at a meeting of the Society of Arts, on May 31st, 1871, by (Maria Shirreff) Mrs William Grey, to whose pioneer labours this narrative will return. Briefly, the facts are familiar, and hardly require recapitulation. The governess in private families, whose position, "as a rule, was unenviable," in the moderate language of Mr Traill in *Social England*, and the measure of whose unenviability is preserved in many vivid novels, from *Jane Eyre* downwards; the "elegant abridgements" (by the same authority), which formed her library of books, and which survive to-day as by-words of in-efficiency; the false standards of social propriety: "it was considered discreditable," says one historian, "that a lady should subject herself to what little of mental discipline may be derived from cooking or making caps"; the whole preparation for complete womanhood, which consisted, *teste* Mr Traill again, in "a steady application to vocal and instrumental music and to the subject of ladylike manners and deportment,"—various proofs might be adduced to the truth of these summary judgments.

We prefer, however, if we may, in a sphere where so much more was owed to unmarried than to married women, to risk the easy ridicule of nieces and nephews, and to cite the half-forgotten "maiden Aunt" of Tennyson's neglected *Princess*. She was a lady, it may be recalled from the prologue (she only receives "a showery glance" in the epilogue), who probably saw a great deal more than she said, and the little that she said was marked by insight and precision. *The Princess*, let us note at the outset, was published in 1847, a year or two (this is important) before the foundation of Queen's and Bedford Colleges, and within a generation of Miss Mangnall's early death; and in the *Quarterly Review* of April, 1869, it was historically described as "the most solid barrier which English wit had erected against the encroachments of the *femme savante*." But the reviewer was reckoning without the aunt. "England," he declared, "is not prepared for either female suffrage or a female Parliament, for women as Poor-Law guardians, attendants at vestries, public lecturers, public speakers, doctors, lawyers, clergy," and so forth. It may be: England's unpreparedness has often been the measure of her success in overtaking it; and the *Quarterly* reviewer of 1869 may have lived (let us hope he did) to see the Reform Act of 1918. So we come back to the "most solid barrier," and to the "maiden Aunt" who helped to break it down.

It will be remembered that "we were seven" at Vivian Place, on that summer's day in the middle of the nineteenth century, when Sir Walter Vivian opened his grounds to "his tenants, wife and child," and "half the neighbouring borough with their Institute, of which he was the patron." One of the seven was the narrator, a college friend of the younger Walter, the host's son, and, earlier that day, he had been diving "in a hoard of tales which dealt with knights." Among those tales was one of a "miracle of noble womanhood," whose "gallant glorious chronicle" he took with him, his finger in the book, when young Walter called him to the park, to join Aunt Elizabeth, sister Lilia, and the rest. "The patient leaders of the Institute" had to take their turn with the others: "Sport went hand in hand with Science; otherwhere pure sport"; but, on the whole, "strange was the sight and smacking of the time"—the time, as we remarked just now, of the foundation of Queen's and Bedford Colleges. Aunt Elizabeth, we suspect, had sent a donation to Frederick Denison Maurice, for, while the lads told of undergraduate exploits, and of their "tutor, rough to common men, but honeying at the whisper of a lord,"

> the maiden Aunt
> Took this fair day for text, and from it preach'd
> An universal culture for the crowd,
> And all things great.

She would have made England a land fit for heroines to live in, and this talk of colleges and crowds "brought,"

says the narrator, "my book to mind." He read out the
tale of the dame of chivalry, so much praising her noble-
ness that Sir Walter, patting Lilia's head, asked, "Where
lives there such a woman now?" Sister Lilia, despite
the caress, was quick, we remember, to that challenge.
"There are thousands now such women," she declaimed,
> but convention beats them down:
> It is but bringing up: no more than that:
> You men have done it: how I hate you all!

Lilia's facts were correct to some extent, whether she
was talking of colleges or schools, for the future Schools
Inquiry Commission, over which Lord Taunton was
to preside, did discover that certain educational endowments had been wrongfully diverted from girls to boys,
and the Women's Educational Union, founded in 1871,
partly in consequence of that Commission's *Report*, and
subsequently merged in the Girls' Public Day School
Company, was gravely concerned to find the means of
replacing those lost endowments. But Lilia did wrong
to hate the men, and her wish to be a great princess,
and "build far off from men a college like a man's,"
was greeted, as we know, with comments of "part
banter, part affection." The banter was ready, of
course, in 1847 and for many years to follow. Our
Quarterly reviewer, in 1869, was pleased to remark,
that "the question has advanced beyond the reach of
banter"; but here, at Vivian Place, twenty-two years
before, Tennyson might reasonably invent the well-
worn coin of boys' laughter at "prudes for proctors,
dowagers for deans, And sweet girl graduates in their
golden hair."

Here, however, Aunt Elizabeth spoke up. "Why
not a summer's as a winter's tale?" she asked, and, if
a summer's tale at all, "a tale for summer as befits the
time,"—the time, again, of sport mixed with science,

and of that converted house in Harley Street. "A little sense of wrong," we are told, "had touch'd her face with colour" as she voiced the demand for

> A talk of College and of ladies' rights,
> A feudal Knight in silken masquerade,—

such talk, for example, though she may not have known it, as an Italian educator, Lionardo Bruni, held in 1405, in behalf of a lady of the Renaissance: "Let religion and morals," he had urged, "hold the first place in the education of a Christian lady," and, secondly, "history, a subject which must not on any account be neglected by one who aspires to true cultivation; for it is our duty to understand the origins of the history and its development, and the achievements of peoples and kings"— not Miss Richmal Mangnall or another. Surely, high among those who felt and interpreted the daughters' need, in the dark age of women's education, we may place Lilia Vivian's maiden Aunt Elizabeth.

Aunt Elizabeth, whom we mention for the last time, had not merely to encounter the affectionate raillery of her male relatives; she was also to find, very soon, that many cultivated women, fully as conscious as she of the demand for women's education, were apprehensive of the innovations. Their objections were based on several grounds. In the last resort, they were attached to the *status quo*: the governesses, after all, were not so bad; it might be difficult to run the house without one; the pupils were certainly learning social manners and elegant deportment; and, since there was a piano in the schoolroom (and musical instruments at that epoch were cheap), why not teach the girls to perform on it? Rather higher in the scale of argument came the reasoned doubt as to the superior advantages of High Schools. Were they not likely to turn out a generation of

girls made to pattern, and, haply, to the pattern of boys?
Chemistry, mathematics and the humanities might
prove perilous, defeminizing studies. These female
candidates for graduation, bemused and probably be-
spectacled, would be fit for nothing but to compete with
men on terms naturally unequal. And, at the top of
the objections, came the *argumentum ad hominem*, or the
question of what a man wants. A young lady's business
was matrimony; would it advance her prospects in that
always overcrowded market to introduce so violent a
change into the course of her preparation for it? "We
bring up our daughters to be wives," cried the opponents or critics of the public schoolgirl, and the Victorian matron was sufficient in her self-esteem. We may
leave it to Mr Lytton Strachey, and to other Victorian
idol-breakers, to reveal the fallacies of that great age;
but Mrs Grey, in her 1871 paper at the Society of Arts,
to which reference was made above, said the first word
and the last word in reply to that particular argument.
"They are not educated to be wives, but to get hus-
bands," she announced, and her dictum, though un-
palatable, was true; so true, that an education for complete womanhood, including wifehood and motherhood,
should they ensue, has been gradually replacing, during
the past half-century, the imperfect instruction in certain limited accomplishments fit for women which was
all that was left at that time—once more, the time of
Queen's College—of the gracious Renaissance ideal[1].

And what was it that Mrs Grey asked for? We shall
come in the next chapter to the more precise aspects
of her work: to what she did, and tried to do, in con-
junction with other women of her time and type. Here,

---

[1] Another stage of this gradual process, which is not to be condemned
merely because it was not born full-grown, is marked by the Board of
Education Report on Curricula, 1923.

however, it is appropriate to note the main lines of her projected reforms, and to observe how conservative they were, in the true sense of that term, how conscientiously they were directed to the expression and fulfilment of women's powers, and how they were founded, historically, on past records of women's achievements. British womanhood, after all—Mr Lytton Strachey would insinuate this more ironically—was not always mid-Victorian in its outlook. The tradition of British public life included Queen Elizabeth and Queen Anne, Lady Jane Grey and Queen Mary of Scotland. Fanny Price at Portsmouth, in *Mansfield Park*, seemed to ask for the High School, which was founded for her descendants by the Girls' Public Day School Company in February, 1882; but *Mansfield Park* was written by a woman, and English fiction, from Sir Philip Sidney to George Meredith, has been truer to the type of the open-air heroine than to that of the *femme larmoyante*, or the *Gretchen* of German sensibility. The restricted conception of women's duties, so fashionable in the middle of last century, was not really native to this country, and our reformers of fifty or sixty years ago were reactionaries rather than revolutionaries: repairers of an educational breach, and restorers of social paths to dwell in.

True, Mrs William Grey was a candidate for election to the new School Board for London, in November, 1870. She published three addresses to the electors in the Borough of Chelsea, and each of them was opened, by herself and her chairman, with an apology for her sex. Then, too, she read that paper to the Society of Arts in May, 1871, and she spoke at a public meeting— a veritable landmark in the history of this movement— at the Albert Hall, in May, 1872. Unfeminine? It would seem so, from her own references to these acts, which were, at least, unconventional at the time. But could there be anything more feminine, more pertinent to the ideals of noble womanhood, than what Mrs Grey actually said? Before the Society of Arts she pleaded for "three points of the educational charter for women: (1) The equal right of all women to the education recognized as the best for human beings" (and women, after all, are human beings); "(2) The equal right of girls to a share in the existing educational endowments of the country, and to be considered, no less than boys, in the creation of any new endowments" (and, after all, a Royal Commission had admitted that such monies had been diverted from girls' to boys' schools); "(3) The registration of teachers, with such other measures as may raise teaching to a profession as honourable and honoured for women as for men" (and the State, after all, was employing women to teach). So far, this modest programme contained nothing to arouse the ever-watchful opponents of women's rights. The most conservative *Quarterly* reviewer could sleep quietly in his bed, without deducing "a female Parliament" from the registration of female teachers and the recognition of women as human beings. But, supposing Mrs Grey obtained the "charter" which she asked for, would the ell invalidate the inch? We may turn to her speech at the Albert Hall, in order to discover more exactly the scope and aim of her projected reforms. The main object of her movement, she said,

was to give united strength to hitherto isolated efforts. They hoped that their schools would be places not only of instruction, but of education in the true sense of the word, and a training of the individual girl, by the development of her mental and moral faculties, to understand the relation in which she stood to the physical world around her: to her fellow-beings, whether as members of her family, her country, or her race; to her God,

the Father and supreme Lord; and to know and perform the
duties which arose out of these relations

(not, therefore, in the first instance, to exercise rights).
But

she believed there was one right of women which they might
advocate incessantly: the right to have their reason trained to
form just opinions upon the circumstances around them, their
sense of moral obligations cultivated to permanent motives of
action. If society was just and wise, it would concede these
demands of women for the good of the Commonwealth. If a
sound education were once supplied, we might dismiss all fear
about the future of this country. A noble manhood was the
inevitable result of a noble womanhood.

Much is written in these days—we have referred re-
spectfully to one of the most distinguished writers—
about eminent Victorians and their faults. Doubtless,
their faults lay thick upon them,—as thick as the dust
on the stuffed birds in Timothy Forsyte's drawing-
room in Bayswater: faults of the time-illusion, which
deemed prosperity eternal, faults of vision and imagination, which exalted property and propriety to the pin-
nacle of virtue and desire; faults of colour, sympathy,
and taste. The survivors of that age have suffered a
rough awakening, and, perhaps, they should not com-
plain. But, at least, they may look back, and may
teach their descendants to look back, when they have
done with reconstructing society, on the ideals which
animated their leaders. Surely, it was no mean am-
bition, on the part of the women of 1870, "to have
their reason trained to form just opinions upon the
circumstances around them." That reason was still untrained in the middle-class daughters of England, when
the war of 1870–71 left its legacy of hate and revenge.
Is it fanciful to say that it was trained only just in time
"to cultivate the sense of moral obligation," in English

mothers of 1914, "to permanent motives of action"?
And, if so, is it not the part of the present generation
to "dismiss all fear about the future of this country,"
and to prove in their new experience that a noble manhood is the result of a noble womanhood? How far
the schools of our Trust have contributed, and will
contribute, to this result, within the limits of their
thirty-eight foundations, the following chapters should
help to show.

CHAPTER II

THE PARENTS' PROVISION

THE Women's Education Union, the short title of the National Union for the Education of Girls of all Classes above the Elementary (the elementary class had been provided for by the State educators in 1870), was constituted in 1871. It disappeared a few years afterwards. Formally, it seems to have been dissolved in or about 1884; but, as in the Holy Roman Empire, the date of its dissolution was later than the date of its disappearance, and it survived, like the Empire, in its offspring,—the Girls' Public Day School Company, founded in 1872, and the Teachers' Training and Registration Society, founded in 1875.

The topics of women's education and of the need of secondary schools for girls had been discussed earlier in 1871 at a Congress in Leeds: a Social Science Congress of the type satirized by Matthew Arnold—so often a gadfly of the Victorians—in a famous passage in his essay on Wordsworth. In this discussion, as in all that went before the actual constitution of the Union, the prime mover was Mrs William Grey. She was the original honorary secretary of the Union, she acted as hostess to its first meetings at her residence in Cadogan Square, her name was selected by the founders of the Maria Grey Training College, and, when she died in September, 1906, her colleagues on the Council of the Girls' Public Day School Trust ascribed, faithfully and gratefully, "the origin of the Trust to her efforts," and added that her "eloquence and energy inspired widespread interest, in the provinces as well as in London, and led to the early formation of numerous country schools."

These praises, amply deserved, are supported by contemporary evidence. In the archives of the Women's Education Union are certain papers, published under its auspices, No. 1 of which was written by Mrs Grey, No. 2 by Miss Mary Gurney, to whose distinguished services to the cause we shall have occasion to come back, and No. 3, dated 1872, by Miss Emily Shirreff, Mrs Grey's sister and coadjutor. "The National Union," said Miss Shirreff, "in forming which Mrs Grey worked for months alone, is still a small body, a poor one, without power, trusting to no assistance from Government, to no influence of party, and yet hoping to do a great work." The two statements illustrate each other: at the beginning, Mrs Grey's lonely work, and her formation of a poor, small body, without power, influence or money, yet sustained by a great hope; at the end of her devoted life, the origin of the Trust traced to her efforts, and the early formation of numerous schools throughout the country attributed to her eloquence and energy.

The lack of friends and funds, to which the Union called attention at the start, was always a matter of regret. "Let it be fully understood," wrote Miss Shirreff, after referring to the fact that the Central Committee of the Union had drawn up a scheme for a public day school in West London, which should be "absolutely self-supporting," "Let it be fully understood that it is not on ground of pride or principle that we repudiate the idea of depending on endowments." It was simply their necessity in being poor. "I confess," she continued, "that I should be only too happy if such a charity as that which founded Eton and Harrow, Westminster and Rugby, and again extends its benefits to the education of men at Oxford and Cambridge, and all the other universities, were extended to girls also. But they have been disinherited too long." Years later, the charity of Dean Colet, who founded St Paul's School in 1509, was extended, after four centuries, to the disinherited girls, and out of the surplus revenue of the Mercers' Company St Paul's Girls' School was erected on Brook Green. But the girls' Eton, Harrow, Westminster and Rugby still await their royal or pious benefactors; and, meanwhile, the Public Day School Company, in which Mrs Grey's Union became merged, by thirty-eight girls' foundations in the course of a little less than twenty years, found a new way of doing the "great work" done for boys at the time of the Renaissance.

"Acting upon these views," ran the concluding words of Miss Shirreff's pamphlet in 1872, "the Central Committee of the Union has put forth its scheme for a Public Day School for Girls, in the South Western district of London, the funds for which will be raised in shares of £5 each, by means of a Limited Liability Company, capable of extending its operations hereafter in various directions, wheresoever schools are wanted."

Bold and novel as the scheme was, the Limited Liability Company, registered on the following June 19th —the Memorandum and Articles of Association were signed at Mrs William Grey's house,—bore, and has always borne, distinct traces of its more romantic origin. The local groups of £5 shareholders have not been unrecognizably removed from the type of the pious founders in the sixteenth century. Their Board of Directors is called a Council; their Council consists of men and women (constitutionally, one woman to two men); their governing body includes a President and Vice-Presidents; and, above all, they enjoy Royal patronage. To this feature, differentiating our Company from commoner concerns in that category, a new paragraph is due.

The first President of the Women's Education Union was H.R.H. Princess Louise, then Marchioness of Lorne, and, since 1900, Duchess of Argyll. The active co-operation in women's efforts of a daughter of the reigning Sovereign was at once a privilege and an inspiration, and, writing neither as biographer nor courtier, but simply as our schools' historian, I may say that their welfare and prosperity have been of constant interest to her Royal Highness. A preliminary meeting of persons interested in the formation of the Union was held, by her invitation, in her dining-room at 1 Grosvenor Crescent; she retained the Presidentship of the Union until its dissolution in 1884, and ever since has consented to act as Patroness of the Trust. The patronage has been genuine and generous. School after school can tell of her gracious presence at prize-givings, at the opening of new buildings in various districts of London and outside it, and at combined gatherings of the schools which have been held from time to time. She visited the (first) Chelsea School on March 28th, 1873. She used her influence on March 16th, 1883, to procure us the signal honour of a speech at the Albert Hall by H.R.H. the Prince of Wales (King Edward VII) and of the distribution of the prizes by the Princess of Wales (Queen Alexandra). At St James's Hall, in 1888, at the Crystal Palace, in 1890, and in 1894, when the vast Albert Hall was again the scene of a combined prize-giving, our Patroness handed the awards[1]. In

---

[1] One or two more Royal days may be mentioned. In 1891 the Duke and Duchess of Connaught visited our Portsmouth school, when her Royal Highness distributed the prizes; in 1900 (May 10th), H.M. Queen Alexandra distributed the prizes again at the Albert Hall, with the late King in the chair (their Majesties were then Prince and Princess of

1912, when, as will appear, it was necessary to appeal to the public for the endowment of a Building Fund, Princess Louise signed the letter to *The Times*, and accepted the Treasurership of the Fund, with his Grace the (late) Duke of Argyll as senior Trustee. These are but a few facts and dates, out of a record extending over more than half a century, and, while they help to illustrate the constant, undeviating kindness which our schools have received from her Royal Highness, they may indicate, too, the personal interest behind the public acts. More than this cannot properly be said, but the presence of Queen Victoria's daughter, first as President and then as Patroness of a movement directed to the provision of improved education for girls, is an invaluable, if silent, reply to the criticisms of that movement as unfeminine or as contrary to the Victorian convention.

The main lines of Mrs Grey's scheme will be obvious by now. It combined, and aimed at combining, two several ideas. The first was the modern idea of a company of shareholders, with limited liability, undertaking the business of building and running schools, which should be "absolutely self-supporting," and which should return a modest dividend on the capital outlay. The second was the ancient idea of reproducing in the commercial surroundings of the nineteenth century the atmosphere of the Renaissance, when pious founders endowed seats of learning with lavish, ungrudging hands,

> Albeit labouring for a scanty band
> Of white-robed scholars only,

and education was an end in itself. Towards this second

Wales); in 1907 (June 14th), their present Majesties, the King and Queen, then Prince and Princess of Wales, took the same parts in the same setting, and were accompanied by Princess Mary.

idea, the Royal President, or Patroness, contributed no merely illusory part, and the Princess was, naturally, supported by an illustrious roll of colleagues. Thus, the officers of the Women's Education Union, according to the *Bulletin* of January, 1873, included, as Vice-Presidents, the Archbishop of Dublin, the Bishops of London, Exeter, and Manchester, Lord and Lady Dufferin, Lord and Lady Lichfield, Lady Antrim, Lord and Lady Napier, the Dowager Lady Stanley of Alderley, Lord Lawrence, Lord Lyttelton, Lord Henry Lennox, M.P., Sir J. Kay-Shuttleworth, Bt., Sir A. Grant, Principal of Edinburgh University, the Dean of Westminster, the Provost of Trinity College, Dublin, the Rt. Hon. H. Austin Bruce, M.P. (afterwards Lord Aberdare), and the Rt. Hon. J. Stansfeld, M.P.

The Central Committee, whose resolution as to founding a school in South-West London has been recorded above, included Mr Joseph Payne of the College of Preceptors, as Chairman, the Dowager Lady Stanley and Sir James Kay-Shuttleworth, and, among others, Canon Parry, Mrs Baden Powell, Mr (later Viscount) Bryce, Miss Buss, Mrs Albert Dicey, Captain (later Sir) Douglas Galton, Miss Mary Gurney, Dr J. M. D. Meiklejohn, Miss Shirreff and Mr (later Sir) Leslie Stephen. It has been observed that, when the parent Union yielded place to the Limited Liability Company, the Royal President became Patroness, the Vice-Presidential officers were retained, and the Central Committee became the Board of Directors, under the new style of Council.

There remained the vacated post of President, and this has been filled successively by the ninth Earl of Airlie (1872–81), son-in-law of Lady Stanley, the first Lord Aberdare (1882–95), the fifth Earl Spencer (1896–1907), and the Marquess of Crewe, our present

President. Some of these names will recur for further notice,—notably, those of Lady Stanley and Miss Gurney, who died respectively in 1895 and 1917, and who were unremitting in service till the end. Here we may add that the Marquess of Lorne, afterwards Duke of Argyll, was an original member of Council, and that Lord Aberdare's daughter, the Hon. Alice M. Bruce, Vice-Principal of Somerville College, was elected to it in 1902.

One more word is necessary in passing in order to do justice to this idea, which is incorporated in the title of a book on *The Renaissance of Girls' Education: A Record of Fifty Years*, published in 1898, and written by Miss Alice Zimmern. The association with the movement of men and women of high rank or otherwise distinguished in public life created a feeling of confidence, which reacted on the class of workers who were the real makers of the new renaissance. Let me quote the testimony of Dr Dorothea Beale, at the annual conference of Headmistresses held in 1906. "A grand work," she said, "was begun by Mrs William Grey and her sister Miss Shirreff—the establishment of the National Union for Women's Education. Their goodness, their high position in society, and their speech (always with grace) disarmed opposition, and led to the formation of the Girls' Public Day School Company." This is how the teachers regarded it: it was a movement of recognition and consolidation; it set the seal of public approval on private efforts frequently warped by misunderstanding or left neglected in obscurity. "From that time"—1874—continued Miss Beale, "scarcely a year has passed without some collective expression of opinion from Headmistresses, without their influence being felt in bringing about schemes for the benefit of Education generally, for improving the position of

Assistant-Mistresses, but, above all, for sustaining a high tone"; and she bore special tribute to Miss Jones, of our Notting Hill School, and to Miss Benson, the first Headmistress of our Oxford School, who "was a burning and a shining light, unsparing in her demands upon herself and others."

The same note—for we are discussing the growth of principles—was struck with great effect, in the resolution moved by Miss Anna Swanwick[1] at an annual meeting of the Women's Union, held at the Society of Arts: "That this Meeting, considering it one of the indispensable conditions of good teaching that the teachers should have received a liberal education extending beyond the school period, pledges the Union to increased efforts towards obtaining the means of such an education for women." Resolutions of this kind, moved up and down the country, and supported by such speakers as Huxley, Seeley, Edwin Abbott, Mark Pattison, and others, inevitably raised the whole matter above the level of controversy and polemics into the serene atmosphere of the *chose jugée*, and gave a buoyancy to the aims of the teachers' profession, which lifted it into the upper air. The status of teachers was raised, and increased efficiency and self-confidence marked and accompanied the rise. The splendid series of Head and Assistant Mistresses on the roll of the Girls' Public Day School Trust, to some of the names upon which we shall come back, was, partly, at least, the result of that note of ideal revaluation struck by the founders at the start.

Next, as to the first idea, the working idea of the whole scheme, from which it derived its practicality,

---

[1] 1813–1899; Hon. LL.D. Aberdeen; sometime President of Queen's College; one of the founders of Girton College; translator of Aeschylus and Goethe's *Faust*.

and to which it owes its success: the shareholders with limited liability. The present directors, or Council, are fully and sorrowfully aware that the shareholders have received no dividend since 1912, and that, in quite recent years, at any rate, this has not been wholly due to lack of profits. A credit-balance of £16,644 was shown in the accounts for 1919, of £12,017 for 1920, and of £2,581 for 1921, and in none of these years was it distributed. The Council preferred to create reserves to meet (1) the expenditure on buildings undertaken after the lean years of the war, and (2) the increases in teachers' salaries in accordance with the Burnham Committee's report, and they were fortunate in each instance in obtaining the Company's assent. Moreover, these after-war measures of prudence do not exhaust the tale of our shareholders' sacrifices. When the Day School Company became a Trust under the scheme of 1906, and was thus enabled, as will be explained in a later paragraph, to satisfy certain conditions, the profit divisible in any year was ordered to be limited to a fixed rate of interest not exceeding 4 per cent. And even this limited return, already cheerfully agreed to by the shareholders, was not always forthcoming. The decision to apply for a State Grant was reached at a period in our history when the original buildings, at least of our earlier schools, were beginning to become antiquated. More accommodation was required, and, particularly, more equipment. Laboratories, gymnasia, and even lavatories were being installed in other schools on a scale very much more generous than had been revealed to our founders in the seventies. "Absolutely self-supporting," Miss Shirreff had said, in that long-ago *Bulletin* of the Union; but since the money originally subscribed by the £5 shareholders had been spent on bricks and mortar at the time, and since pupils' fees barely sufficed to pay the costs of staff and maintenance, how were the little grandchildren of the Trust, the children of the daughters for whom the call had been made, to be provided with the more luxurious appurtenances which a new generation found essential?

By raising fees, was an obvious reply, and it did not escape the anxious Council's attention. But what would parents get for the higher fees, which they could not get better elsewhere, or, if not better, at least seeming better by the meretricious standards of yesterday? For here another factor intervened, due to social conditions before the War, and, even more particularly, before the Third Boer War and the Liberal revolt in 1905. There were more wealth, more luxury, more gaiety, and, perhaps, less desire to bring up children at home, in those far-off days which we called *fin-de-siècle* than there are in these strenuous times; and, if the fees at our schools had been raised beyond a certain level, varying a little according to locality, but nowhere more than moderate, they might have excluded the sisters of many boys at public schools, and yet not have attracted the richer pupils at fashionable boarding-schools or in the competent hands of newly certificated private governesses. In both directions, perhaps, we were penalized as pioneers. The newer schools, for which we had served as models, were better equipped than ours, and mothers from well upholstered drawing-rooms viewed our shabby furniture and fading distemper with surprise, while the teachers, whom we had helped to learn their worth, assessed it higher than our resources could afford. For some years, our numbers declined, our premises deteriorated, our difficulties increased; and, despite the accretion of the State Grant, the 4 per cent. interest was not payable. The historian would gladly pass over these lean and anxious years, and would be content to mark them with a tribute, first, to the loyalty, sympathy, and almost passionate forbearance of all the mistresses in the schools, and, secondly, and hardly less amply, to the constant patience of the shareholders, with whose part in our history we are now more immediately concerned. The situation was frankly explained in the letter to *The Times* of July 6th, 1912, to which reference was made above, and which was signed by H.R.H. Princess Louise, by Lord Crewe, as President of the Trust, by Lord Lansdowne, the Bishop of Peterborough, Lord Reay, Lady Jersey and Miss Gurney, as Vice-Presidents, by the Rev. Prebendary the Hon. J. S. Northcote, then Chairman of Council, and by Mr Wyndham Dunstan, Chairman of the Building Fund Appeal Committee. We had postponed that letter as long as we possibly could. To some of us, its wisdom was always doubtful; to all of us, its eleemosynary character was disagreeable; but the time came when we had to choose between "going to the public" and failing to provide a public need. With this brief reference to a hard decision, the following extract from the letter is self-explanatory:

"The cost for providing suitable school buildings" (we wrote, after an account of our foundation and record), "has been hitherto defrayed from capital subscribed by parents and others interested in the higher education of girls. On this capital the Trust has paid a low rate of interest; the main income, derived from school fees, being devoted to maintaining the general educational efficiency of the Schools. In recent years the financial task of the Trust has become more and more difficult. It is true that the Trust receives from the Board of Education some aid in the form of grants based on the efficiency of the teaching, which have assisted in obtaining the services of specially qualified teachers in certain subjects. But this assistance is far more than counterbalanced by the increased cost of education, the necessity for augmenting the salaries of teachers, and the cost of equipment, especially in connection with instruction in Science, Art, and Domestic Economy. Even in face of this greatly increased expenditure on education, the Council of the Trust has considered it of the first importance to keep the fees of the Schools at as low a level as possible, having regard to the many calls on the limited means of the parents with whom the Schools of the Trust are so largely concerned. The school fees, which have been increased in recent years, now average about £16 a year[1], and it has not been found desirable or practicable to increase them further. It is now necessary to provide new buildings for some Schools and to improve the buildings of others. The Council of the Trust feels that the strictly educational demands made on their limited resources have become so great that they must raise a Special Fund for this purpose, and they therefore ask all those who realize the importance of the work they are doing to assist them in obtaining a sum of £50,000, to be devoted exclusively to building purposes."

It was characteristic of the kindness of our Patroness that replies to the Appeal were to be addressed to her Royal Highness at Kensington Palace.

Such, then, were the two ideas, combined in the original scheme, and continued, however imperfectly, from 1871 to this day: the idea of a limited company, subscribing capital and earning dividends, and the idea, succinctly, of the Renaissance, as expressed in the endowment of education. That the two have been completely harmonized, it would be vain to contend, in the near presence of our chequered annals of vexatious regulations imposed by the Grant-paying Board, of a depleted exchequer in periods of decaying walls and increasing rivals, of teachers' salaries soaring to a figure, by no means high in abstract altitude, but sometimes disproportionate in the perspective of the incomes of the parents of their pupils, of the tide of population ebbing away from a district where we had once founded

[1] The present (1923) average is £24 a year.

a prosperous school, and of no power to raise a rate to build new schools in populous districts, of overdrafts, mortgages, sinking-funds, and the rest of the items in the annual balance-sheet, which successive generations of shareholders have, willingly or reluctantly, but always most generously, adopted. Yet, always through these difficulties, which caused particular pain to a particularly able and conscientious chairman of our Finance Committee, the late Mr Aldred W. Rowden[1], it may be claimed by a successor to that chair, which has never been a seat of roses, that "the main income" of the Trust, as stated in our letter of 1912, has been consistently "devoted to maintaining the general educational efficiency of the Schools." This was the undertaking in 1872; we venture to claim its fulfilment fifty years after.

The course of this chapter has taken us a long way from that long-ago year, when Mrs Grey had the unique satisfaction of giving shape to women's education. A way back may, perhaps, be found through a "Memorandum on the Annual Income and Expenditure of the Chelsea and Notting Hill High Schools, and on the present Income of the Croydon High School," prepared by Sir James Kay-Shuttleworth, and printed for the Council's use on December 4th, 1874. (The Chelsea School, as will appear in Chapter IV, was opened in January, 1873, Notting Hill in September, 1873, and Croydon in September, 1874, thus enjoying, at the date of this Memorandum, the exceptional luck of income without expenditure.) There were 285 pupils in the three schools, and their fees for the Autumn term just concluded had amounted to £1598. 2s., which would yield an average fee for the

---

[1] Member of Council, 1911 to 1919; Chairman of Finance Committee, 1914 to 1919; author of *The Primates of the Four Georges.*

schoolgirl's year of £15. 7s. 8¼d.[1] Repressing a parent's natural sigh at the frugal expense of fugacious years, we may observe more sternly that the ratio concerns us more nearly than the rate. Sir James Kay-Shuttleworth very properly pointed out, that

> In order to ascertain how much of this income is available for the purposes of tuition in each school, it is necessary to state (1) the amount of rent, rates, and taxes, (2) the outlay in the year ending 1st September, 1874, in housekeeping and cleaning, advertising, fuel, gas, and expenses included under the head of Petty Cash. (3) It is desirable that each school should, at an early period, pay interest on the Capital expended in founding it, and also a rate per cent. for depreciation, as well as for the redemption of Capital.

Proceeding on these lines, he calculated that the annual *cost* of a pupil at Chelsea School was £18. 14s. 5¾d., while the annual *fee* was £15. 6s. 4½d. (a trifle below the average of the three schools), showing an annual *loss* of £3. 8s. 1½d. per pupil. At Notting Hill, the return was a little brighter, showing an annual *profit* of 5s. 7¼d. on each of its 118 pupils. These calculations were made without provision for the "desirable" items in Sir James's preliminary statement. Thus, the capital sunk at Notting Hill was at that date £1560; "5 per cent. for interest," he wrote, "5 per cent. depreciation, and 10 per cent. as a redemption fund, would amount to about £2. 12s. per pupil," or, roughly, ten times the amount of the annual profit. Allowing for the necessary growth in the general charges of administration (law, repairs, inspection, examination, etc.), Sir James reached the conclusion that the cost of tuition should be kept to within £8 per pupil, leaving

---

[1] This sum included extras, etc., excluded from the £16 average referred to in 1912 in *The Times* letter, above.

£4. 10*s.* for administrative expenses, and £2. 17*s.* 8*d.* for interest, etc.

The problems, it will be seen, were the same, and were present to the founders from the start, though their range and complexity have grown to more serious proportions. The bulk of our shareholders to-day are the successors or assigns of the original subscribers to the Company. The first enthusiasm, necessarily, has waned. With Council Schools in every district, to the cost of which they contribute by law, and with the old "eloquence" forgotten and the old "energy" defunct, which helped to build their schools, they cannot be expected in every instance to accept without murmur or regret the present financial position. The parents in law of education cannot share the transports of its first parents. But the Memorandum of 1874 affords satisfactory proof that the shareholders' point of view has never deliberately been postponed either to the pupil or to the teacher. Through all increases and encroachments, in the incidence of which, whether to admit them or to resist them, our Council has taken a due part, we have tried to preserve that ratio between fees, salaries, administration, and the interest on and protection of capital, which was discussed, when our third school was founded, by so eminent an educator and public servant as Sir J. P. Kay-Shuttleworth[1].

In order to complete this portion of our survey, it should be added that, in 1906, when the Girls' Public Day

---

[1] Sir J. P. Kay-Shuttleworth, Bt. (1804–77), was the first Secretary of the Committee of Council on Education (1839–49). He gave valuable assistance to Mrs Grey's efforts during the early period, 1871 to 1875–76, and was the first chairman of the Council of the new Company, references to his connection with which will be found in his *Life and Work* by Mr Frank Smith (Murray, 1923). The present writer is indebted to Lord Shuttleworth for the loan of the Memorandum quoted in the text.

School Company was converted into a Trust, a scheme was devised, which was revised in 1912, and finally approved by the Board of Education, by which elaborate provision is made to wind up the Trust as a Limited Company not later than 1956. By that time the mortgages should have been discharged by means of the fixed Sinking Fund. The property of the Trust will then be free for the realization of shareholders' claims, up to but not beyond the amounts originally subscribed by them, and any surplus remaining, after the elimination of the shareholders, is to be handed over to an educational Trust approved by the Board of Education. A hundred "new" shares of 1s. each, carrying each a thousand votes after January 15th, 1956, such votes to be exercised according to the orders of the Board of Education, were created specially for this purpose.

The above is a very brief account of a very long and complex legal arrangement between the Trust and the Board of Education. Its effect, briefly, will be to transfer the schools of the Trust from the Limited Liability Company, formed under the leadership of Mrs Grey, to a new Trust without shareholders. The date fixed, 1956, is determined by financial causes, chiefly connected with the repayment of the mortgage-debt. Thus, it will happen, so far as can be foreseen, and so far as provision can be made, that the Company, which was registered in 1872, and received dividends till 1898, which voluntarily decided in that year to limit its interest to 4 per cent., in order to qualify for the Grant of the old Science and Art Department, which proceeded in 1906 to devise a scheme for its conversion into a Trust, and which completed that scheme to the satisfaction of the Board of Education in 1912 (since when the statutory rate of interest has been withheld, either by necessity or by choice), will be retransferred in 1956 —eighty-four years after its incorporation—into a purely educational Trust. The two parent-ideas, the idea of the Renaissance and the idea of the nineteenth century, may be combined in the second half of the twentieth century, in a form not foreseen by our founders, but not out of harmony with their intention.

CHAPTER III

THE TRUST'S VALHALLA

IT is time to recall the famous men and women most prominently associated with the subject of this chronicle. Some have flitted across the stage, shedding light reflected from other scenes; some have been connected with the movement without interruption for many years. To all alike, the present bearers of the burden, the present wearers of the founders' mantle, desire to convey a meed of praise.

In the first category may be mentioned the encouragement given at the start by great leaders of thought in the last century. Thus, Huxley, for example, wrote to *The Times* on July 8th, 1874, on the topic of women's education in the following circumstances. Miss Sophia Jex-Blake had approached him in 1872, "to ask his help for herself and the other women medical students at Edinburgh." He was unable to accede to this request and when, two years later, Miss Jex-Blake was rejected at the Edinburgh examination, "her papers were referred to Huxley, who decided that certain answers were not up to the standard." Accordingly, he wrote to *The Times* to say:

As Miss Jex-Blake may possibly think that my decision was influenced by prejudice against her cause, allow me to add that such prejudice as I labour under lies in the opposite direction. Without seeing any reason to believe that women are, on the average, so strong physically, intellectually, or morally, as men, I cannot shut my eyes to the fact that many women are much better endowed in all these respects than many men, and I am at a loss to understand on what grounds of justice or public policy a career which is open to the weakest and most foolish of the male sex should be forcibly closed to women of vigour and capacity.

So far, *The Life and Letters of T. H. Huxley*[1]. A week earlier, on July 1st, 1874, Huxley had been in the Chair at a Girls' School meeting in St John's Wood. There he said, that experience proved that success in every station of life was less the result of moral and intellectual strength than the exercise of patience, industry and temper, qualities very much dependent upon healthy organisms. Both men and women, he added, stood on an equality in the matter of patience, industry and temper, and, as the capacity for education rested on these qualities, he could discern no reason why bringing up the education of girls to the same level as boys should be calculated to endanger their physical welfare. Fighting prejudice as we were at every step of our progress, so grave a pronouncement by so weighty an authority was timely and welcome.

It was a great thing in these days to be taken seriously, and to win the goodwill of responsible men. Girls' education—let us be clear about it—was reinvented by women's wit. "However much men helped by collecting funds," writes Professor Archer (*Secondary Education in the Nineteenth Century*, p. 247), "by giving lectures, and by sharing in the business management, it was women who determined what women's education was to be"; and he cites the essay by Miss Wolstenholme in *Women's Work and Women's Culture*, edited by Josephine Butler in 1869, as "fairly representative of women's views," and the kernel from which the reforms were enucleated. But, true and vital as this is, women alone could not have carried their cause, or would never have carried it so quickly to a successful issue, if they

[1] By his son, Leonard Huxley. Macmillan. vol. II (1903), p. 140.

had not been able to rely, at their meetings and gatherings, on men of mark and eminence in the public eye, such as Huxley himself; Mark Pattison; Abbott, the Headmaster; J. R. Seeley, the historian; Sir James Kay-Shuttleworth, first chairman of our Council, and Charles S. Roundell, who succeeded him; Douglas Galton (1822–99; K.C.B., 1887); the sixth Lord Lyttelton (1817–76; F.R.S., 1840; Chief Commissioner of Endowed Schools, 1869), whose work on the Endowed School Commission proved of so much value to education; W. F. Cowper-Temple (1811–88; Lord Mount Temple, 1880; Vice-President of Committee of Council on Education, 1857–8); the genial and kindly Sir Joshua Fitch, H.M.I.; Joseph Payne (1808–76; first Professor of Education in this country, by appointment at the College of Preceptors, 1872); James (Viscount) Bryce[1], Leslie Stephen, and others, who all rallied round the movement at the beginning. Our successive

[1] Girls' secondary education owes a very special debt to the late Lord Bryce. He and Mr (later Sir J.) Fitch were both among the Assistant Commissioners on the Schools Enquiry Royal Commission, which reported in 1868, and whose Report was followed by the passing of the Endowed Schools Act, 1869. The inclusion of girls in their terms of reference was due to their own courage and to women's pressure from without. "Its framers so completely forgot girls that they forgot to exclude them" (R. L. Archer, *Secondary Education in the Nineteenth Century*, p. 244). Bryce and Fitch were particularly useful in dealing with this extension of the Commission's work, and Miss A. Zimmern (*op. cit.* p. 47) justly says that "Mr Bryce's recommendations are of special interest, since they mark out the lines on which the chief reforms have proceeded.' On Nov. 3rd, 1913, when a Dinner was held at the Savoy in aid of our Building Fund (see pp. 18 and 24, above) Lord Bryce was an honoured guest and an effective speaker.

Among other men of note who have served on our Council may be mentioned in passing: Canon Bell and H. W. Eve, past Headmasters; Sir Henry Craik, K.C.B., later M.P. and P.C.; Sir Alfred Lyall, Lord Reay, F. W. Buxton, R. G. Tatton, Douglas Close Richmond, William Latham and Sir Buxton Morrish. The list is not complete, and, anyhow, *dux femina facti.*

Presidents have been mentioned above, both dutifully and gratefully, and a line should be added here to commemorate the successors to Kay-Shuttleworth and Roundell in the responsible chairmanship of the Council of the Trust. It was held from 1879 to 1897 by Mr W. H. Stone, who died in the latter year. Our next and excellent Chairman was the late Sir William Bousfield, who held the office till March, 1910, a few weeks before his death. He was succeeded by the Rev. Prebendary the Hon. J. S. Northcote, a son of the Earl of Iddesleigh, and a man whose conscientious devotion to duty rivalled his great father's chief characteristic. Mr Northcote held the post through the difficult period of the war, and resigned at the beginning of 1920, shortly before his death on June 5th, when he was succeeded by our present Chairman, Mr Maurice Llewelyn Davies.

Before passing from the men to the women, a share of the meed of praise is due to the name and memory of Andrew McDowall, first Secretary (1874–1909) of the Day School Company. I remember him only as an old man, with a mind which was a storehouse of memories, and with a method so exactly trained to the complete discharge of his duties that the impact of the curiosity of a new member of Council made as little impression as an india-rubber ball on a cushion. In those days, not long before his retirement at Christmas, 1909, after nearly thirty-six years' service to the Trust[1], Mr McDowall's best work had been done. It dated from early in the seventies, when the new venture had

---

[1] His excellent successor is Mr A. Maclean, Barrister-at-Law, who was Assistant Secretary, 1904–09. His two immediate predecessors in that post (Mr L. J. Morison and Sir Edmund Phipps, C.B.) became respectively head of the Pensions Department and Principal Assistant Secretary at the Board of Education.

quite recently taken shape, and his personal interest in education, which was both wide and wise, grew in the course of time to a body of accumulated experience, which proved of the utmost use to successive governors of the schools. He was only not the "permanent Civil Servant" because there were members of Council who over-lapped his appointment and his resignation; but he represented effectively the best traditions of such a permanent official, in his constant care to improve his organization of the increasing business of his post, in his sense of direct responsibility, and in his love for his work. He was virtually a colleague to his employees on the Council and to the headmistresses outside, and, with many scholarly avocations to occupy his leisure, he liked to revisit, in his later years, the ghosts of the past. Lady Stanley of Alderley, "*grande dame* of the Victorians," as he remembered her in middle life, Miss Gurney, with "a more logical mind" than anyone he had ever met, and as generous as she was wise,—these and others moved before him, as he looked back from the plains to the heights, where he had walked with them in the morning.

So we come to the *grandes dames* themselves[1].

The sisters Shirreff have already been mentioned. The elder, Emily Ann Eliza, was born in 1814, and died unmarried in 1897. She took a leading part in the foundation of Girton College and the Froebel Society, as well as of the Women's Education Union. Like her sister, Mrs Grey, author of *Last Words to Girls*, Miss Shirreff was an early writer on education. Her published works include *Intellectual Education, and its Influence*

---

[1] Mrs Reid, founder and benefactor of Bedford College, Frances Mary Buss, and Dorothea Beale, the great Headmistresses of the North London Collegiate and Cheltenham Colleges respectively, do not enter directly into this chronicle.

on Women (1858), *The Kindergarten* (1870), and she was joint author with her sister of the celebrated book *On Self Culture* (1850). The younger, Maria Georgina, was the wife, and at an early age the widow, of William T. Grey, grandson of the first and nephew of the second Earl Grey. Born in 1816, she lived till 1906, thus enjoying the happiness of seeing the fruition of some of her best hopes, and conferring on those who followed her the privilege of greeting her as a pioneer. She was a very effective public speaker, at a time when women on the platform were rare, and, as we noted above, she was a candidate in Chelsea in 1870 for the newly constituted School Board for London. She did not obtain election, but the experience which she gained proved of much service to her in her future work; and her speeches, which were issued in pamphlet form, helped by their wise and quiet eloquence to break down the prejudice against women members. Her paper at the Society of Arts (May 31st, 1871) marked an epoch in the history of the progress of female education, and every one of our schools, from the initiation of the first at the Albert Hall in May, 1872, is conscious of owing a deep debt to the really affectionate care and constant thought of Mrs Grey. She was the true author of the movement, and its guide and counsellor for more than thirty-six years.

Two, and only two, original members of the Women's Union and its child, the Day School Company, share these praises with Mrs Grey. The one is Henrietta Maria, daughter of the thirteenth Viscount Dillon, and known after 1869, on the death of her husband, the second Baron, as the Dowager Lady Stanley of Alderley. The other is Mary Gurney. Lady Stanley died in her eighty-eighth year in 1895, and Miss Gurney in her eighty-first in 1917. With her passing, there

PLATE II

THE DOWAGER LADY STANLEY OF ALDERLEY 1880

passed away the last notable figure among the pious founders of our schools.

In devoting a few lines to the memory of these two great women, I am fortunate in the fact that Miss Gurney herself wrote a memoir of her friend, the Dowager Lady Stanley, which was reprinted in pamphlet form from the *Journal of Education*, April, 1895. Twenty-two years later, when Miss Gurney died, it seemed desirable to commemorate her life and work in a pamphlet of similar scope, and my colleagues asked me to write it. I obtained some of the help which I required, and, though the resulting "impression and tribute" was inadequate and imperfect, this pamphlet, too, however deficient in value, is available for the present chapter.

A sense of paradox sometimes occurs at the record of women so well educated as Henrietta Dillon, Mary Gurney, Emily and Maria Shirreff, and the rest (including in that category the headmistresses whom they were so fortunate as to employ) in the dark age which preceded the *Renaissance of Girls' Education in England* —dated by Miss Alice Zimmern[1] in 1848, the year of the foundation of Queen's College, Harley Street, and the year after *The Princess*. A partial explanation lies in the fact that the new movement was, strictly, a renaissance,—a revival, or renewal, in other words, of ideas which had slumbered for a while, but which had not been disused in particular instances. And in the instances particularly of Miss Dillon and Miss Gurney, there was a certain likeness, even at an interval of thirty years, in the tastes and training of the girls. Lord Dillon, in his daughter's childhood, was living in Italy: in winter, in an old palace on the left bank of the Arno, in summer, in one or another villa in the sur-

[1] See p. 20, above.

rounding hills. There his daughter acquired "that perfect command of the Italian and French languages
which was so charming and valuable throughout her
life." Mary Gurney was born in Denmark Hill, living
afterwards at Lavender Hill and Putney, till her father
and stepmother moved to Tyndale Lodge, Wimbledon
Common, a "spacious, old-fashioned house," where
Mr Percy Matheson told me he remembered her, "remarkable then, as always, by her striking face and
character." But she, too, became a lover of Italy, at
first by study, then by travel: "only to be there was
a delight," her sister told me in after years, and she
published many translations from Italian, French, German and Spanish literature. Mary Gurney, too, was
a born teacher, as her younger step-sisters remember,
and one of them, at least, "wept floods of tears at giving
up lessons with Mary." The renaissance of girls' education, like its historical prototype, was to bring Italy
and her storied past to England: *ecce, Græcia trans-
volavit Alpes*; but, meanwhile, an intimate knowledge
of foreign languages, literatures and countries, and an
innate love of teaching, proved an adequate preparation
in the few for the fountains to be unsealed for the many.

In 1826, at nineteen years of age, Miss Dillon married
Mr Edward John Stanley, a rising Whig politician,
only five years her senior, who filled various Government offices while M.P. for North Cheshire, and who
was raised to the peerage as Lord Eddisbury in 1848.
Two years later he succeeded to the Stanley barony[1],
and from that time he and Lady Stanley resided at
Alderley Park.

Lady Stanley's "interest in education," we are told,
"began from the date of her marriage, as she at once

[1] The two baronies are now merged in the older one of Sheffield of
Roscommon.

began the study of Rousseau's *Emile*, Locke's *On the Human Understanding*, and other standard works, having in view the education of her own young children." In London, despite her social duties as a political hostess, which she performed with rare brilliance and success, she visited schools and even taught in them, and helped to found an industrial school (the Maurice Girls' Home) in 1867, in consequence of her connection with St Peter's, Vere Street, during the incumbency of the Rev. F. Denison Maurice. Her interest in girls' secondary education was largely due to the same influence: "though many have watered and tended the plant," said Archbishop Trench (1854), "the vital seed in which it was all wrapped up, and out of which every part was unfolded, was sown only by him" (F. D. Maurice). Lady Stanley was one of its first gardeners; she was an early governor and visitor of Queen's College, and assisted in obtaining its Royal Charter in 1853. Between that date and 1878, when she attended to present an address of thanks, signed by nearly 2000 women, to Lord Granville on the opening of all the degrees of London University to women, Lady Stanley took a leading part in public movements of this kind. Her "Personal Recollections of Women's Evolution" were published in the *Nineteenth Century Review* in August, 1879. Girton College, University Extension, the Drawing Society and her own parish schools in Cheshire, were among other objects of her interest and enterprise.

Thus equipped, Lady Stanley's accession in 1871 to the Women's Education Union, and her subsequent place on the Council and among the Vice-Presidents of the Girls' Public Day School Company, proved a source of immense strength to Mrs William Grey and her coadjutors. It was not merely, or chiefly, Lord

Stanley's public position, though this lent a prestige to the movement; it was mainly Lady Stanley's personal character, her genuine and vivid appeal to the best faculties of mistresses and girls, her driving and organizing ability, her social gifts and acquaintance, and her enthusiasm for the cause, which made her an outstanding personality on a Council filled with notable men and women. Miss Gurney observes that she "carried out some of her own views as to the importance of special branches of education, by the offer of prizes." Botany and English essays were her particular selection: she "read all the essays herself, marked her criticisms on them, and then took advice as to the final award." But she gave advice as freely as she took it; a fine and mature judgment, supported by the experience stored in a retentive memory, seems to have been a prominent characteristic, which impressed and inspired all her colleagues. Very properly, a photograph from the picture painted of her by Sir William Richmond hangs in each of our schools, where her memory is held in honour.

And Mary Gurney herself, Lady Stanley's "most important ally," as Mr McDowall remembered her, and "the most influential member of the Council"; of whom "no one ever knew," he told me, "all she gave to help poor promising scholars"; whose strong face and remarkable brown eyes always made her an imposing figure in the recollection of Mr Matheson, in his capacity as an Oxford Schools Examiner; whose "gifts and kindnesses to Girton are too numerous to mention in detail," by the testimony of the late Dr E. E. Constance Jones, Mistress of Girton, 1903–16; whom our Council commemorated at her death, in words written by Mr R. G. Tatton, and as true to-day as in our hour of bereavement, "In paying homage to Miss Gurney's great character and services, the members

PLATE III

Miss MARY GURNEY 1894

of the Council would wish to add a warm tribute of
affection. She was in truth one of the most lovable of
women. Her beautiful and entirely unselfish nature,
her unfailing sympathy and a wonderful tenderness rare
in so forceful a character, made it impossible for those
who knew her not to love her": no record of the Girls'
Public Day School Trust can do full justice to Mary
Gurney, who, with all her wide interests and culture,
all her intellectual and material resources, all her enjoyment of hospitality and travel, devoted herself for
forty-five years—from 1872 till her death in 1917—
to the daily business and weekly meetings of the schools.
And, in the widest sense of a fine word, her benefaction
did not end with her life. All that she gave in willing
service of heart and hand and mind, all the easier
sacrifice of her modest worldly substance, return to her
a hundredfold to-day; and, though the schools which
she founded be replaced by State schools of a newer
type, though the personal touches which she valued
yield to dissolving regulations, though the girls who
liked to please Miss Gurney pay homage to a more
impersonal code, still her example survives from the old
time into the new[1].

One little trait may, perhaps, be added, as typical of
the spirit of our *grandes dames*. It happened sometimes,
as remarked in the last chapter, that the Council de-

[1] Miss Gurney, characteristically, after helping schools and scholars
financially all her life, bequeathed her shares in the Company and
£500 for a Scholarship Fund to the Trust.
    Among other women members have been the Lady Frederick
Cavendish; Miss Jane Harrison, the Hellenist; Mrs Lecky, wife of the
historian, and Mrs Henry Grenfell, who died at a great age in 1923,
and whose daughter, Miss Maud Grenfell, is a present member of the
Council. Another honoured present member is the Hon. Lady Digby,
who succeeded Miss Gurney in the chair of the Education Committee,
and is a repository of the best traditions of the schools.

cided to close a school. The Secretary would whisper,
"After all, it's business," and the reluctant directors
would acquiesce. But I think Miss Gurney never voted
for such a resolution. She would not oppose it at the
last, but to vote for it would have seemed to her like
infanticide.

An efficient, even a super-Council, as a governing
body of schools, is excellent and admirable, and worthy
of commemoration at a Jubilee. But the pre-requisite
of any school's success is an efficient head of its teaching
corps, and the Girls' Public Day Schools were fortunate
in finding super-heads at the beginning. Not even the
spell of Royal magic, symbolized by Princess Louise,
nor all the enthusiasm and eloquence of Mrs Grey,
Lady Stanley and Miss Gurney, nor the utmost forbearance of shareholders, would have availed without
the headmistresses. It is time, then, to invoke their
noble shades.

Late in 1922, out of correspondence arising from
this book, I was fortunate in making acquaintance with
a very young old lady of 81, who had twice been offered
the headmistress-ship of our Chelsea (South Kensington) School. "When refusing the first time," she wrote
me, "at a salary of £200, I said I did not think the
right kind of person would come forward for a fixed
salary of £200. I said the offer ought to be, either
£250 or £200 *plus* a capitation fee for every pupil over
a hundred. But my own refusal had nothing to do with
salary. I was too happy, prosperous and successful in
my Gower Street School[1]." The writer of this letter,
Mrs (Constance) Bolton, was later headmistress of our
Nottingham and Liverpool Schools successively, preceding Miss Hastings at the one and Miss Huckwell

[1] In connection with Bedford College, London; subsequently closed,
as outside the scheme of foundation.

at the other, and her recollection of conditions fifty
years ago was interesting and illuminating. Apart altogether from questions of salary, in which the Burnham
Scale is as significant as the Plimsoll Line to navigators,
her memory confirmed the impression which every
historian must feel, of the strong individualism of that
period. It occurred to me, while she was talking of old
times, old faces, and old problems, to compare, not the
details which she recalled, more and more exactly as
she proceeded, but the general outline which she
evoked, with the "Draft, dated 4th August, 1922, of
the Regulations for Secondary Schools, England, 1922
(excluding Wales and Monmouthshire), proposed to
be made by the Board of Education, under Section 44
of the Education Act, 1918 (8 and 9 Geo. 5, c. 39)."
The changes are all for the better, of course: they
always are, since progress, too, is regulated; but the
upward curve has been very rapid in the last half-
century. "I said I did not think," etc.; "I said the
offer ought to be," and so on. So, Mrs Bolton to
Mrs Grey, the employed to the employer, towards the
end of 1872; and how, I wondered, as she pecked at
her memories, like a bright bird among autumn leaves,
would Mrs Grey's successors to-day deal as directly
with a Mrs Bolton *de nos jours*. "Subject and without
prejudice to any contract of employment existing on
the first day of August, 1922, the Headmaster or Headmistress must not be paid wholly or partly by means of
capitation fees"; "the rate of fees must be approved
by the Board as suitable"; "the School must be conducted by a Governing Body acting upon and in
accordance with a scheme or minute or body of written
regulations which states its constitution and defines its
functions both as regards responsibility for general
control and as regards immediate responsibility (in-

cluding that of the Headmaster or Headmistress) for the conduct of the school, and which is approved by the Board." So, these Draft Regulations of 1922, with "the approval of the Board" recurring like a minatory refrain.

Two facts have been inevitable in this process. First, the provision of rates and grants in aid of Secondary Schools has marched too quickly for the competition of schools founded without that aid[1], and these have had to conform, *tanto quanto*, with the regulations formed for their juniors; secondly, "the approval of the Board" (if we may use this just phrase as a catch-word), with its veiled appeal to taxpayers and ratepayers, by whom, in a democratic country, that approval, ultimately, is signified, restricts inevitably the initiative of a Governing Body, so approved, and the delegated liberty of action of the headmistress whom they appoint. Pursuing this reasoning for a moment, though expressing no opinion on the facts, it follows that past headmistresses of the Girls' Public Day Schools will have had much less routine labour, much less of the business of education to transact, and have had more time at their disposal to teach, and to devise methods of teaching, and to devote themselves severally to the welfare of their school, as to that of a domestic concern, undistracted by the claims of outside authorities.

Perhaps the measure of their undistractedness was too big at the start. Sir James Kay-Shuttleworth seems to have thought so, if we may judge from a memorandum which he circulated among his colleagues in July, 1874. There he pointed out, that "the number of ladies eligible as Headmistresses of High Schools is small, and the Council have to depend on their own unaided inquiries

[1] "Trusting to no assistance from Government." Miss Shirreff 1872. See p. 15, above.

in determining their fitness for their responsible positions." He contrasted the means available for forming
such judgment with the means available to the governors
of boys' schools: "The headmasters have usually attained the highest honours of their University; have
sometimes passed through a distinguished career in the
discipline and instruction of their college, . . . and bring
with them proofs that they may be entrusted with an
authority subject only to the general control of the
Governing Body." But what did the Girls' Schools
Council really know of the work of their Schools? "One
or two members of the Council," wrote Sir James, "do
visit individual schools; but such visitation is liable to
prolonged interruption, . . . and it cannot be expected
to have a systematic and an official character." There
were two schools of the Company at that date (Chelsea
and Notting Hill), and it was about to found its third
school at Croydon. "The distance of that school," continued Sir James, "will interpose a new obstacle to that
degree of knowledge of the internal organization of its
schools, which it appears to me expedient that the
Council should possess." "I conceive," he went on in
a later paragraph of this important Memorandum,
"that whenever a High School is established at a distance, a local Committee with some functions will
necessarily exist. It will then be necessary to maintain
communication between this Committee and the Council,
and to have the means of co-ordinating the management of the more distant schools with that of those
which are nearer."

Sir James Kay-Shuttleworth was quite right, and
local committees were empanelled for most of our distant schools. But in practice, as a fact, there was very
little for them to do. Our first headmistresses, though
selected from so small a field, proved equal to the con-

fidence reposed in them, and our first Council, though
a body of amateurs, proved adequate and efficient. This
was, perhaps, the luck of the beginners; and the forms-
and formula-ridden methods of to-day, when individualism has yielded to socialism, and very considerable
powers have been delegated by the central Council to
very strictly constituted local Committees, are no doubt
as much better as they are more precise. At the same
time, admitting and even condoning the improvement,
it is salutary to recall the kind of headmistress who
was produced by the more elastic conditions of yesterday.

May I rely for a moment on a review given by Miss
Beale at the Annual Conference of the Headmistresses'
Association as recently as 1906? She recalled then the
first meeting of "eight Headmistresses at Myra Lodge
(Miss Buss's home), December 22nd, 1874," at which
she had presided, "lying in great pain on the sofa, and
taking only a feeble part in the discussion. I little
thought," she remarked, "that I should be allowed to
address a Conference which more than thirty years after
numbers over 230 members." Accordingly, she did
well to look back as well as forward. "We who belong
to secondary schools," she remarked, "have been happy
in escaping from the troubles which beset those schools
which receive Government grants. So far" (alas, not
much farther!) "secondary schools have been allowed
some individuality. I think we may give thanks for
the 'liberty of prophesying' that we have hitherto enjoyed. I rather dread the results of the absorption into
Trusts of the great School Companies." (Our partial
absorption followed very soon!) "We have escaped
payment by results, and interference from Inspectors,
some of whom are able to see the body but not the soul
which moves it." And, "when the secondary schools,"
she asked, "are absorbed into the national system, and
orders are issued to us from the Education Depart-

ment" (long since the Board of Education), "shall we be told . . ., shall we be forbidden . . .? These are matters which seem to press for answers."

They have been answered by reams of regulations, none of which it is our present business to discuss; but when Maria Grey, Henrietta Stanley and Mary Gurney meet their headmistress friends in the Elysian fields, it is possible that they turn with a wise smile from the printed evidences of "the Board's approval," and seek out again for their delectation the joy of service beyond its rules.

Harriet Morant Jones, who, as we shall see in the next chapter, opened the Notting Hill High School, the second of the Company's foundations, with ten pupils on September 16th, 1873, may be cited as a type of those headmistresses. She was born in Guernsey, in 1833, and, on her mother's side, was of French and Huguenot descent. She gained some early teaching experience in her native island, where she started a school, and she was forty years of age when, with considerable diffidence, she accepted the appointment to Notting Hill. This she held till 1900, tranquilly ruling her school, while it expanded in number from its first half-score to over twenty score, and then laying down her burden and living as tranquilly in retirement. She died on a night of enemy air-attack—October 20th, 1917—having passed the great age of 84.

Dorinda Neligan (1833 to 1914), the first headmistress of our third school, is even more typical of the class of women who made our schools in the nineteenth century. Her father was Lieutenant Thomas Neligan, who served with distinction in the Peninsula War, and Dorinda, his fifth daughter, like Queen Victoria, was always proud to be a soldier's child. She served with the Red Cross in France from August, 1870, to March, 1871, being in sole charge at Metz during the siege, and, though she "hated war," her spirit did not desert her in old age, when she took part in the forgotten battles for women's suffrage. A brave and brilliant personality, Miss Neligan brought to the Croydon High School, of which she was headmistress from 1874 to 1901, qualities eminently suited to the constructive work of educational reform. That Miss L. Gadesden and Miss Cossey, later headmistresses in our schools, were trained under Miss Neligan at Croydon, is a part of the debt which we owe to her work at that school. Her fine face and presence are shown in the life-size painting of her at the school, and her voice was equally fine. She spoke with readiness and incisiveness, succinctly, with a great command of words. A head mistress who knew her well writes to me: "Her courage, frankness and large-heartedness were admirable, and she both possessed, and developed in others, independence of character, moral courage and intellectual honesty. Socially she was a power, and she was absolutely without snobbishness. I remember Mr Roundell speaking of her on the Croydon High School platform as 'a woman of the world,' and there is no doubt about it that she worked with men easily and ably as few women of her profession could do at that period. Her war experience probably helped her. The firmness of the foundation she laid at Croydon is shown by the steady advance of this School under Miss Leahy, a loyal successor."

What is the secret of the success of Miss Neligan, Miss Jones and contemporary headmistresses, who were born in the dark ages and yet irradiated them with light? Partly, and making full allowance for the partiality of their pupils' evidence, the answer must be stated negatively. They were not hampered by regulations. They were not hemmed in by a code. They had room to grow and to expand, to make experiments, even to make mistakes, since these were not made at the expense of the public. They correspond to the Thomas Arnold of boys' schools, but they had this advantage over Arnold and his peers, that they were breaking new ground. Miss Buss was born in 1827, Miss Beale in 1831, Miss Neligan in 1833, and these three teachers had much in common. "In this year" (1864), says the historian[1], "Miss Beale resorted to a change as regards the hours, which had hitherto been arranged on a plan usual in boys' schools. She now experimented with a morning lasting from nine to one o'clock, broken by a half-hour's interval, keeping the afternoon for individual music lessons and such extras. The plan was adopted by Miss Buss in the following year, and became the standard allotment of hours with the schools of the Girls' Public Day School Company." Lucky women, to experiment with a morning! Their successors may hardly experiment with five minutes. Again, and by the same token: "the average schoolmistress thinks more about methods than the average schoolmaster. The school is a more civilizing influence. There is no tradition from the ages of barbarism to wear down. Headmistresses looked to what girls naturally were; headmasters have looked to what boys after a hundred years' tradition of idleness, bullying, housing in hovels, and worship of physical strength, had become." And once more: "Miss Buss's school was to a large extent the model of the 'High Schools,' as the schools of the (Girls' Public Day School) Company are commonly called. . . . Miss Buss was indeed a great personality. . . . All her life through she was able to absorb new ideas. . . . She wished headmistresses to have the same independence from their governing

---

[1] *Secondary Education in the Nineteenth Century.* By R. L. Archer, Cambridge, 1921.

bodies as headmasters" (which partly suggests an
answer to the dubieties of Sir J. Kay-Shuttleworth, and
partly invites comparison with the conditions of to-day).
Once more, *les neiges d'antan*, the winter snows of
yesteryear! To have time to *think* about methods, instead of decocting their statistics on to ruled foolscap;
to look to what girls *naturally* are, instead of forcing
them to what they must legislatively become; to be able
to *absorb new ideas*, instead of turning a deaf ear to their
urgent voices, and postponing their consideration to
distant years of retirement: the first generation of our
headmistresses enjoyed opportunities of freedom denied
to their successors to-day, and we watch with some
disquiet and anxiety the rapid transition of the type
from the teacher to the administrator. There may be
a consequent gain in uniformity, even in economy and
efficiency, the twin aims which bureaucracy tends to
miss; but some of us cannot help believing that initiative, liberty, and leisure, are also parts of the equipment
of a successful head. The meticulous State regulation
developed under the presidentship of Mr Fisher may
be satisfactory in ensuring that every child has his
chance of education, and that no preference is given to
any class; but the history of the foundation of Girls'
Public Day Schools illustrates another aspect of the
social problem, and proves that, when a class has been
excluded from the benefits of education, it supplies
them spontaneously from its own resources, and builds
the schools, and discovers the staff. If, in a jubilee
review of that history, we have been tempted to dwell
too affectionately on the good sowing or the good luck
of amateurs, and have been a little irked or even irri-
tated by the tapes and buttons of professional authority,
let it be our excuse, in submitting to it, that our Valhalla
resounds with the praises of the great women who

toiled alone in barren plains, now the sites of populous cities.

In the Cambridge lectures on *Education in the Nineteenth Century*, referred to in chapter I, Sir Michael Sadler indited some passages on "National Education and Social Ideals," which apply with no less force to the century in which we are labouring. "By means of an elaborately organized system of higher education," he said, "it seems possible to overestimate the intellectual susceptibility of large numbers of people of mediocre talent, without adding much to the sound stock of initiative or practical judgment possessed by the nation." This might be written in letters of fire across each year's Education Estimates. Again: "Neither in complete freedom from central control; nor in any extreme form of State or municipal monopoly, are we likely to find the right balance of educational policy." This was said in 1901; we may endorse it after more than twenty years. And, lastly, and more closely to the ideas which inspired the founders and heads of the Girls' Public Day Schools half a century ago:

We need constantly to remind ourselves that the rising generation has not to be prepared merely to pass examinations, or for an imaginary life of ideal ease and intellectual recreation, nor yet on the other hand merely to play a boisterous part in struggles for private gain; but that the chief object of education should be, while fitting boys and girls for the tasks and duties of practical life, to preserve intact for them, amid the repeated assaults of claims and cares which arise from the fact of daily work and from the results of philosophical inquiry and from the play of competition far beyond individual or national control, as much as may be of childlike faith, of intellectual reverence and homage, and of gaiety and truthfulness of mind.

I know no words more appropriate than those closing this paragraph to be inscribed as the epitaph of a Mary Gurney, a Dorinda Neligan, or a Harriet Morant Jones.

CHAPTER IV

THE SCHOOLS

WE founded thirty-eight schools in all, between 1872 and 1901. Some, for various reasons, have been closed; some have been transferred to other authorities; twenty-five are flourishing to-day; and if we prick a map of England with the dates of the thirty-eight foundations we shall obtain a bird's-eye view of our distribution of activities. We went as far north as Carlisle and Newcastle, as far south as Brighton and Portsmouth, as far east as Ipswich and Norwich, as far west as Liverpool (two) and Swansea. We sowed Greater London with seats of learning—in Blackheath, Clapham (two), Dulwich, Hackney, Highbury, Putney, South Hampstead, Streatham Hill, Sydenham and Wimbledon. In London itself, we founded the Chelsea (Kensington), Notting Hill and Maida Vale (Paddington) Schools; just outside London, beyond the south-eastern suburbs, Croydon, Bromley, and Sutton; further still, in the same populous direction, Tunbridge Wells and Dover; in other directions, Nottingham, Oxford, Bath, Newton Abbot, Gateshead, Sheffield, Shrewsbury, Birkenhead, Weymouth, York.

Glance at the markings on the map, and then recall, if you will, the reflection in the mirror of fiction of the conditions of social life in some of those places in the generation prior to our schools. Jane Austen, perhaps, is a little early, but the unlit girlhood of children in the fading splendour of old houses in Bath and "The Wells" can be imagined from a dozen or more novels of the years before 1875 and 1883, when we brought the torch of education to these quiet cities successively. The more prosperous and busier life of professional and tradespeople's families in big cities like Liverpool and Sheffield offered little satisfaction to the craving for higher opportunities which stirred, unanswered, in the bosoms of idle daughters in opulent homes. "Outside the family circle," says the historian of *Social England*[1], writing of 1865 to 1885, "women had not much to look for. A little intellectual effort went a long way"; and it was during those years precisely that the Princess, Mrs Grey and Miss Gurney, accompanied or followed by the men of business, with their ledgers and share-certificates, went through London, its suburbs and the provinces, on their educational mission.

We may recall the terms of the effective resolution, moved by Mr Cowper-Temple (Lord Mount Temple), seconded by Mr (Sir) Joshua Fitch, and carried unanimously, at the Albert Hall in 1872:

That the first scheme of this Company, namely, to open a public Collegiate day school for girls in South Kensington, in which provision will be made for the training of teachers, meets with the approval of the meeting, and deserves the support of the inhabitants of the district, both by taking shares and entering pupils.

It was all there, *in petto*, from the beginning. The provision for the training of teachers was a feature of the scheme at the start, because the Council of the Company fully realised the urgency of this reform. Nothing is more remarkable, indeed, in all the annals of our schools, than the great number of headmistresses who have been selected by outside bodies from our staffs[2]. The approval of the *meeting* was sought, not the approval of the Government—a phrase which we

---

[1] Cassell. Vol. VI, p. 643.
[2] Lists will be found at the end of most of the separate school-histories below.

met in the last chapter,—because it was for the inhabitants of the district to decide whether *this* supply satisfied *that* demand; whether the ideas of social reform conformed with economic law. And such approval could only be expressed individually, by the active, practical operations of "taking shares and entering pupils": not merely by registering a vote for the representative of the less mischievous of two policies, not merely by paying a rate, or complying with a taxcollector's requisition, not merely by obeying compulsion, imposed ultimately, by the majority without, but by the voluntary, inside acts of subscribing shares and sending children.

So, we come to the schools themselves, in the order of their foundation, with the exception of those which have been closed, and which are collected together at the end of the present chapter.

I. KENSINGTON

The Chelsea, or South Kensington School, now famous as the Kensington High School, and especially famous for its music, was founded, as we have seen, in 1872, and was opened at Durham House on January 21st, 1873. Six years later, it was removed to 152 and 154 Cromwell Road, and its present premises in St Alban's Road, Kensington, were occupied in 1888.

This bare statement of bald facts leaves a good deal to the imagination, and the imagination likes to play—with the assistance of Leigh Hunt, L'Estrange and Mr Reginald Blunt[1]—on the early history of Durham House, and the associations with which its old walls were crowded, when Miss Porter first met her twenty

---

[1] In *The Old Court Suburb, A Village of Palaces,* and *Paradise Row,* respectively.

pupils on that Tuesday morning, in January, 1873. We
know that Mrs Grey and Lady Stanley gave long and
anxious consideration to the terms of the lease of their
venture; that Durham House was rented by a Dr Wilson
from the Earl of Cadogan on an expiring tenancy, and
that the neighbouring houses were doomed to demoli-
tion. We know that it was suitable to its purpose, with
two staircases and eighteen rooms, some of them particularly large, exclusive of kitchens and the usual
offices, and that it stood in its own grounds; and we
may conjecture that the surveyor's report was so attractive to the Council of the Trust, that they took the
risk—after all, it was their first school, and the enterprise might not be successful—of having to look for
another house in a few years' time. All this is ordinary
enough: the common romance of a new undertaking,
with all the enchanting vistas that open out of parch-
ment bonds. But Durham House was more than the
first venture of a pioneer Company founding girls'
schools. Durham House had a long past as well as a
short future, and the Renaissance spirit which we have
noted as an element in the Company's constitution—
or, at least, in the character of the *grandes dames* who
gave it a habitation and a name—may have been stirred
by the appeal of the old walls, the old gardens, and one
tenant of olden times. We read of the "eleven large
windows facing Burton Court," of the "massive door
with carved side-jambs," of the "grand staircase, seven
feet wide, and large, lofty, panelled rooms." It was "a
place of importance," says another writer, "and stands
back behind a broad gravel road and green sward."
These architectural qualities of breadth and height and
symmetry, this atmosphere of massiveness and large-
ness, made it a suitable house in which to train little
girls from Chelsea to noble thoughts and big ideas.

But Durham House had been inhabited by Sir Isaac Newton. "The great astronomer came here from London" (Chelsea was not in London in 1709–10), "in consequence of an attack of the lungs," and lived there, we hope to his benefit, for a couple of busy years, partly employed in correcting proofs of the *Principia*. He who overheard the harmonies of the spheres might not reluctantly have consented to the sounds of children's voices in his study. It was not used by us as a schoolroom for the first time. Already in 1805, for a period of thirty years, more or less, a succession of French schoolmasters, MM. Cruiseau and Clément and Dr Grave, had been turning out good French and classical scholars from Newton's old seventeenth-century house, with its convenient playing grounds.

We had to leave it in 1879, for the two houses in Cromwell Road, where the rent was six times as high, and there was no garden. Meanwhile, Miss Porter left us to go to Bradford, and was succeeded in 1875 by Miss M. A. Woods. She, too, left us in the following year, to become Headmistress of the Clifton High School, and was succeeded by Miss Bishop, whom we transferred, with her consent, to our own school at (VIII) Oxford in 1879, which she left in 1887 in order to take up the Principalship of Holloway College.

Her successor at Kensington was Miss Hitchcock, whose term of office as Headmistress lasted from 1879 to 1900, and on whose capable shoulders fell the burden of the double flitting,—first to Cromwell Road, and afterwards to St Alban's Road. A tribute of gratitude should be paid to her for the success with which she carried the School through those busy twenty-two years of growth and progress.

In 1900 we had the advantage of appointing as Headmistress Miss Ethel Home, a lady whose mathematical attainments are matched, as is so often the case, by an aptitude for music, which amounts in her case to genius, a word often misapplied, but here used appropriately. In 1921 Miss Home celebrated her majority as Headmistress, and the tributes paid her on that occasion were rendered in grateful recognition of the remarkable growth in the numbers of the pupils, of the School's unique reputation for music-teaching, of its Music Training Department, and of the large number of warm friends whom it had attracted during Miss Home's reign. Special reference is made in another chapter to the distinguishing feature of this School, which, whenever a display of music is given in the School, astonishes and delights all beholders, and which has brought Miss Home into requisition as a lecturer, as a member of committees, and, inevitably, as an author, in many directions of brilliant and useful work.

PROMOTIONS FROM THE STAFF

HEADMISTRESSES

Miss E. C. J. Abbott	Municipal Secondary School, Cardiff
Miss D. M. Bakewell	Batley Grammar School
Miss Bedford	Girls' Grammar School, Middlesbrough
Miss Benton	(IX) South Hampstead
Miss Bishop	(a) (VIII) Oxford (b) Principal of Royal Holloway College (c) Principal of St Gabriel's Training College
Miss Bott	Head of Warrington Training College
Miss A. B. Clark	Hulme Girls' School, Oldham
Miss Coombe	Liverpool Institute Girls' School
Miss Duirs	(a) Weymouth High School (b) (XXVIII) Sutton
Miss Field	Whalley Range High School
Miss Higgs	Roan School, Greenwich
Miss Limebeer	Pendleton High School
Mrs Luxton	(a) (VI) Nottingham (b) (X) Brighton
Miss Musson	The Abbey School, Reading

Miss Prebble	{(a) Truro High School {(b) Kendrick Girls' School, Reading
Miss Thatcher	Secondary School, Bath
Miss A. Woods	Head of Maria Grey Training College
Miss M. A. Woods	Clifton High School
Miss Young	Valparaiso High School

II. NOTTING HILL

Our second venture was at Notting Hill, on the north side of Hyde Park, in a neighbourhood similar in some respects to that of the Chelsea School opened in January, 1873. On the following September 16th, Miss Harriet Morant Jones met the first ten pupils in the building which we had taken in Norland Square, and which had been used as a boys' school. Thoroughly suitable for its purpose, it possesses, among other assets, a fine and commodious Hall, which has frequently served for conferences and gatherings. The lack of a convenient playground was gradually met to some extent by alterations designed by Miss Gavin, the second Headmistress (1900–8), who added the gardens of two adjoining houses, acquired to meet the growth in numbers, to the space available at the back of the main building. Playing-fields at Acton and Ealing, which have been leased in order to supply the same lack, have been brought closer in recent years by the hire of a motor char-à-banc for the transport of the girls.

Tribute has been paid in the last chapter to the pioneer work of Miss Jones, whose reign as Headmistress lasted from 1873 to 1900, and who stamped on the School the impress of a great personality and the seal of a permanent tradition. Her retirement coincided with that of her Second Mistress, Mrs Withiel (Miss M. Andrews), who was the first woman permanently appointed to the post of H.M. Inspector of Secondary

Schools, and who remained in office as Staff Inspector till 1922. Her name is still held in affectionate regard by the "old girls" of Notting Hill, where her labours were complementary to those of Miss Jones. In 1920 a sum of £1000 was collected by the Old Girls' Association (established as long ago as 1885), and funded in a Leaving Scholarship which they presented to the School in memory of its first Headmistress, Miss Jones. Miss Gavin, transferred from (XXIX) Shrewsbury, reigned till 1908, when she was re-transferred to (XXI) Wimbledon, where her principal work for the Trust lay. Her successor, Miss Steele, transferred from (XXIII) Portsmouth, left the service of the Trust in 1910, in order to assume the Headmistress-ship of the Grey Coat School for Girls, at Westminster. She was succeeded at Notting Hill by Miss Paul, whom, as will appear, we transferred to (V) Clapham at the end of 1912, since when the Headmistress of Notting Hill has been Miss M. M. Berryman, M.A.

I am conscious of dropping into a catalogue, and of omitting the punctuation-marks. The record of the School under Miss Jones, in her exceptionally long reign, was one of increasing success in the External Examinations, to which, in the period following the *Report* of the Schools' Inquiry Commission of 1869, it was good policy to direct attention. Parents, staff, and pupils were ignorant of the standard that girls could reach, and at that time it was of first importance to secure a standard that could impress the public. Staff and girls spared no pains to get good results, and worked together in a united effort which settled into a school tradition. The Headmistress, a hard worker herself, possessed among her many admirable qualities the invaluable gift in an administrator of selecting her assistants wisely, and then leaving them largely to their own initiative. The results in examination lists were very remarkable. From 1879 to 1890 the School entered large numbers of girls for the Cambridge Junior and Senior Locals, with the result that the School obtained the best Senior girls eight times and the best Junior three times. In 1888, when the first really valuable scholarships were open to girls—the three St Dunstan Exhibitions of £100 a year for three years,—a new chance was given to Notting Hill. In the first four years, eight of the twelve Exhibitions fell to Notting Hill girls. In 1918 an "Advanced Course" in Modern Studies was introduced. The general culture which this gives to all girls of post-Matriculation stage, whether going up to the University or not, has been much appreciated by both parents and pupils. Moreover, Notting Hill High School has sent up a great number of girls to the Universities. During the time of the first Headmistress, girls who went on to Cambridge, Oxford and London, and secured distinguished positions in those Universities, not only adorn the School roll, but in many instances have won distinction in various fields of work in after life. The high reputation for scholarship has been steadily maintained since 1900, and not least since 1913, when Miss Berryman's reign began. The acquisition in 1922 of a very pleasant boarding-house at St Michael's, 3 Lansdowne Road, has considerably facilitated the solution of the problem of accommodation.

PROMOTIONS FROM THE STAFF

HEADMISTRESSES AND OTHERS

Miss Adams	(a) Secondary School, Eastbourne
	(b) High School, Macclesfield
Miss Adamson	(XXIII) Portsmouth
Miss Aitken	High School for Girls, Pretoria
Miss Andrews	(XIII) Maida Vale

Miss Beevor	(XXVII) Carlisle
Miss Blake	(School unknown)
Miss Clark	$\begin{cases}(a) \text{ (XX) York} \\ (b) \text{ (VI) Nottingham}\end{cases}$
Miss M. Collin	City of Cardiff High School
Miss J. Connolly	Haberdashers' Aske's School for Girls, Hatcham
Miss A. J. Cooper	Edgbaston High School
Miss Hall	Pontefract and District High School
Miss Vernon Harcourt	County School, Chelmsford
Miss Heppel	(XXV) Bromley
Miss Hodge	(XXV) Bromley
Miss Hollings	Edgbaston Church of England College
Miss V. Home	Preston High School
Miss K. Jex-Blake	Girton College
Miss Lefroy	Streatham College for Girls
Miss Emily Lord	Founder of the Norland Institute
Miss Mason	County Intermediate School, Bangor
Miss Munro	Chesterfield High School
Miss Nimmo	King Edward's Grammar School for Girls, Birmingham
Miss A. A. O'Connor	$\begin{cases}(a) \text{ (V) Clapham Middle School} \\ (b) \text{ (XXIV) Clapham High School}\end{cases}$
Miss S. Allen Olney	(XVII) Blackheath
Miss Purdie	$\begin{cases}(a) \text{ Exeter High School} \\ (b) \text{ Sydenham Secondary School} \\ (c) \text{ (XIII) Maida Vale}\end{cases}$
Miss Slater	(XIII) Maida Vale
Miss Stoneman	Park School, Preston
Miss Storey (Mrs T. W. Smith)	School for Officers' Daughters, Bath
Miss Tovey	(XXXI) Streatham Hill
Miss Weld	(VII) Bath
Miss Williamson	Princess Helena College, Ealing
Miss M. Anderson	H.M.I. of Factories
Miss K. T. Wallas	$\begin{cases}(a) \text{ Member of the L.C.C. Education Committee} \\ (b) \text{ Girton College Council}\end{cases}$
Mrs Withiel	H.M.I., Chief Staff Inspector, Board of Education

BENEFACTIONS

The Old Girls' Association (an association which figures prominently in the history of the School) has given prizes and gifts at different times, of which the chief are:

An Annual Prize to be competed for by the whole School for different subjects, chiefly General Knowledge.

A very valuable gift of books for the Library, given in remembrance of Miss Andrews' work at the School.

Miss Shirreff, one of the earliest Members of Council, could almost be described as a founder, by her generous help in securing the present site.

Oak furniture for Library and Headmistress's office, presented by Miss Eccles, who was also generous in giving books to the Library, and at various times gave Scholarships to girls tenable in the School.

ENDOWED SCHOLARSHIPS:

"Harriet Morant Jones Scholarship," awarded every three years.

"Ramah Ezra Scholarship," awarded every three years.

ENDOWED PRIZES:

"Irene Graham Memorial Prize," an Annual Prize given by Mrs Graham.

"The Frances Wood and Dorothy Chick Memorial Prize," an Annual Prize given by Mr and Mrs Chick, in memory of two daughters.

The late Sir William Meyer, G.C.I.E., bequeathed a sum of money for an Annual Prize.

III. CROYDON

Our Croydon School was opened with eighty-eight pupils at a house called "The Chestnuts" in North End, on September 14th, 1874. It was removed to its present site in the Wellesley Road in May, 1880, and may reasonably claim to have fulfilled the ideal delineated by

Dr Tait, then Archbishop of Canterbury, who laid the foundation-stone on July 12th, 1879. Our Company, he said, "was the first to bring home to English families the highest intellectual education, conjoined with the quiet and sanctifying influences of home." The eighty-eight pupils of fifty years ago have been multiplied nearly eightfold; a Junior School has been opened at Purley, and other houses have been taken, but the original ideal has been faithfully preserved by the only two Headmistresses of the School—Miss Neligan, whom we revisited in the Trust's Valhalla in the last chapter, and Miss Leahy, the present Headmistress, who succeeded her in 1902. The time, fortunately, is not yet to pay Miss Leahy the full tribute due to her brilliant reign, but that time may safely be anticipated by the remark that her name will rank in a future history with those of our greatest headmistresses, in moral influence and academic success.

Princess Louise visited the School in 1895, on the occasion of its twenty-first anniversary, and the Marchioness of Crewe distributed the prizes in 1912. In 1914, a scheme was approved by the Board of Education, under Article 22 of their Regulations for Secondary Schools, by which the management of the School was transferred from our Council to a joint committee of eight governors, four of our own and four from the Croydon Borough Council. The Croydon scheme was the first of a long series, which has gradually brought us into relations with Local Authorities in various districts, and which, while it has proved the value of the work which our Trust initiated, has taken much of its control out of our hands. The Borough grant was, of course, the lure, but we were extraordinarily fortunate in obtaining, together with the grant, the co-operation of local governors of the type of the late Sir Frederick

Edridge, and of his colleagues. Sir Frederick, speaking at the School in 1914 said, that

The Croydon Borough Council were unanimously of opinion that the suggestion (of joint-government) should be fallen in with, on the ground that the School was a great educational asset to the Borough, that, therefore, it ought not to be lost, and that a little touch of local colour would, if possible, improve its condition.... The status of the School could not possibly be improved upon, nor could its curriculum.

The services of Sir Frederick Edridge, till his death in 1921, were ungrudgingly devoted to maintaining the standard and traditions of the School, which has twice shown the way to the builders of education in Croydon: first, with its foundation in 1874, and, again, at its re-birth in 1914. The School has been fortunate, again, in attracting the generous confidence of the present chairman of its governors, Mr Howard Houlder, who, among many acts of kindness, bought two adjacent houses, and let them with their gardens to the School at a nominal rental. His help has been invaluable, too, in the expansion of the buildings in 1923.

There are two Advanced Courses at the School (Modern Studies and Mathematics), recognized by the Board of Education; and its fine record at the Universities, including two Cambridge Wranglers, 124 University degrees, and more than fifty College scholarships, and its flourishing associations for French, History, Science, and other studies, indicate, to those who know, the progressive success of the work which has been done under Miss Neligan and Miss Leahy, and a series of Assistant Mistresses, among whom it would be invidious to make selections, and whom it might prove tedious to enumerate in full.

High in the list of Trust Schools' Benefactions is the Clough Scholarship for Croydon girls, founded in 1895 out of money raised by entertainments and subscriptions, and conferring a scholarship of £30 a year at Newnham College.

PROMOTIONS FROM THE STAFF

HEADMISTRESSES

Miss E. Cannings	$\begin{cases} (a) \text{ (XXIX) Shrewsbury} \\ (b) \text{ (XVIII) Liverpool} \end{cases}$
Miss A. F. Cossey	(XXIII) Portsmouth
Miss H. Drew	Colston Girls' School, Bristol
Miss L. Gadesden	(IV) Norwich
Miss Gardiner	(XXVII) Carlisle
Miss M. Gardiner	The High School, Blackburn
Miss F. Johnson	Bolton High School (Lancs.)
Miss E. M. Julian	$\begin{cases} (a) \text{ (XXVI) Tunbridge Wells} \\ (b) \text{ Principal, Avery Hill Training Coll.} \end{cases}$
Miss M. S. Ker	Withington Girls' School, Manchester

LECTURER

Miss K. Jefferies Davis Peterborough Training College

IV. NORWICH

For our fourth school we went farther afield, and on February 22nd, 1875, the High School at Norwich was opened, under the Headmistress-ship of Miss Benson (Mrs McDowall), whom we moved in the following November to our new foundation at (VIII) Oxford.

Norwich, with its generous motto, "Do thy best, and rejoice with those who do better," has been a successful and a happy school, under Mrs McDowall, Miss Wills, Miss Tapson (Mrs Arthur Helps), Miss L. Gadesden (from (XXII) Newton Abbot), and, since 1907, Miss Gertrude M. Wise, who came to Norwich from (XXIX) Shrewsbury. The Bishop of Norwich distributed the prizes in 1883, and H.R.H. Princess Louise in 1896, and the after-activities of the prize-

M

winners and others have been particularly notable. Fifteen University scholarships—twelve gained since 1900—have fallen to Norwich girls; twice the Kaisar-i-Hind silver medal has been awarded to Old Norwich Girls in India; and at home there is practically no important field of work in the city, in times of peace as well as in the years of war, without the participation of Norwich High School Old Girls, who not only maintain a flourishing Old Girls' Society, but through it subscribe towards an exhibition to be awarded annually in the School.

The School has maintained a cot at the Jenny Lind Hospital for Children continuously for thirty-one years, and the money for this purpose, amounting to considerably over £1500, has been raised by entertainments, sales of work, and dramatic performances. Amongst the most notable of the latter have been very beautiful productions of Chaucer's *Knight's Tale*, the *Alcestis*, *Iphigenia in Tauris* and the *Two Gentlemen of Verona*.

It is not fanciful to ascribe a part of these successes, and of the spirit which has informed them, to the *genius loci* of the School buildings. After about two years, the School was moved in 1877 into the premises which it has since occupied. These are at once commodious, beautiful, and of historical interest. As long ago as 1250, when a Chapel and a "Hospital" were built by a John le Brun, the site in Theatre Street has been an important one, and has been occupied by noted buildings. In the fifteenth century, the Hospital and Chapel had become by the generous gifts of benefactors a noble College known as the College of St Mary in the Fields, and its common seal displayed this motto, encompassing a lily, the cognisance of the Virgin:

De campis nomen Virgo dedit addat omen.

A merchant's mark in stone, impaling the arms of one Robert Browne, Mayor of Norwich in 1454, was found in front of the School during archaeological excavations in 1901 and this, now hanging in the School Hall, was probably placed in the church belonging to the College by one who was a descendant of the original founder—Le Brun.

After the Dissolution the property passed into the hands of more than one noble family, who used it as a private dwelling-house, and it was sold, in 1753, by the last of these, the Hobarts, of the family of the Earl of Buckinghamshire, to a Company, on whose behalf Thomas Ivory, a famous East Anglian architect, designed and erected a theatre on one part of the site, and Assembly Rooms on another.

To this fine artist we owe the beautiful proportions of some of the rooms, and the magnificent examples of decorative plaster work on walls and ceilings. It is in truth a splendid specimen of a Georgian building.

This building (Assembly Rooms) was acquired by the Girls' Public Day School Trust in 1877 and, by subsequent purchases on both sides of it, the greater part of the buildings on the site of the original college are now incorporated in the School.

One especially interesting feature is a crypt, under the present chemical laboratory, which almost certainly formed part of the original college.

These associations have made for steadfastness and tradition, and have encouraged the pupils to look for and to spread beauty in their daily life and character. The School takes a unique place in its educational area in Norfolk, and impresses all its visitors with a sense of high aims consistently achieved.

PROMOTIONS FROM THE STAFF

HEADMISTRESSES

Miss E. Greene	(a) H.M.I.
	(b) Carlton Street Secondary School, Bradford
Miss H. Greene	Principal of Mme Österberg's Physical Training College, Dartford
Miss E. Hughes	High School, Kobe, Japan. (S.P.G.)
Miss E. Lloyd	County School, Penarth
Miss A. C. P. Lunn	(a) (X) Brighton
(Mrs J. H. Doncaster)	(b) (XIV) Sheffield
Miss Primrose	(a) (XX) York
	(b) H.M.I. (occasional)
Miss A. Varley	Principal of Training College, Saffron Walden
Miss M. A. Vivian	High School, Newport, Mon.
Miss G. M. Wise	(a) (XXIX) Shrewsbury
	(b) (IV) Norwich

V and XXIV. CLAPHAM

I come to a school which imperiously cries for a superlative, and yet it is difficult to know which superlative to choose. Perhaps the right epithet is wonderful; for, indeed, there was something like a touch of magic in the growth of the Clapham High School out of a mixture of types, into a single, homogeneous pattern of educational effort and efficiency.

One name particularly is connected with the second foundation of our Clapham School. "It is not," writes a correspondent, whose memory covers many years, "as the chief among great Headmistresses that her name is to be mentioned, but as the conqueror of obstacles which seemed insuperable." "The effect of her presence and personality," writes another correspondent, likewise from personal recollection, "was almost magical. I do not think there ever was such a rapid growth in the history of the Schools; there certainly has never been anything like it since." With these evidences in front of him, the fact that Mrs Woodhouse is to-day an honoured colleague on our Council must not deter the historian of our Clapham School from putting her name in the forefront of its record, confident that time will justify what her own modesty might resist. And out of many eloquent tributes to Mrs Woodhouse's work at Clapham—a work of reconstruction and rebuilding, intellectual as well as (even more than) physical—I can select none more convincing, or worded with better knowledge and more skill, than that of Miss Agnes S. Paul, her immediate successor in the Headship, and herself a Headmistress (1912–17) of rare and gracious ability, whose resignation through ill-health was very deeply deplored.

"As Mrs Woodhouse's immediate successor," she has written me, "I could, perhaps, best appreciate how deep was the stamp of her personality on the school as I inherited it: and also I perhaps more than others could (by a sort of 'ex pede Herculem' calculation!) estimate from her government of her own special province what her services to education as a whole have been, and are.

"That quick perception of the essential—the lightning dart of her mind on to the spot, whether it was of weakness to be guarded against or of strength to be seized upon;—her elasticity and adaptability, alike to learn from the past and to shoot forward into the future—these, I suppose, would have brought her success in any big undertaking. But in such a human setting as a great school these gained immensely in value and effectiveness from the presence of other qualities. Mrs Woodhouse has, for instance, always been an extraordinary judge of character (the staffs she continuously collected round her have been a proverb—a regular nursery of headmistresses!)[1] and with that

---

[1] As will appear *s.v.* (XVII) Blackheath, the long and distinguished reign of Miss F. Gadesden at that School was similarly remarkable for the number of her assistant mistresses who were appointed to head-mistress-ships.

judgment and power to *see* went the wisdom not to speak always of what she saw, and the warm and deep sympathy which never saw unkindly."

Yes: it has been a wonderful School, at any rate, since 1898. Mrs Woodhouse (1898–1912), Miss Paul (1912–17), Miss Annie Escott (1917–21): a succession of great Heads, each of whom has made her mark in the School, which the Council have placed with confidence in the hands of Miss Barratt, who was appointed in 1921. A special word is due here to Miss Escott, whose death on April 22nd, 1921, was a loss, not only to Clapham and to the Girls' Public Day School Trust, but to English education as a whole. *The Times* newspaper, on the following April 28th, expressed this double sense of loss in language worthy of its subject.

The news of the death, after a severe operation, of Miss Escott, Headmistress of the Clapham High School, and formerly Headmistress of the Sheffield High School, will be received with sincere regret throughout the educational world.

Educated at the Sheffield High School and Firth College, she was a colleague under Mrs Woodhouse at Sheffield for several years. The simplicity and strength which were marked characteristics of her girlhood were retained in full measure throughout her career. Her wide sympathy and her excellent teaching powers made her universally beloved. During her assistant mistress-ship she showed much organizing ability. She was chosen by the Council of the Girls' Public Day School Trust to succeed Mrs Woodhouse at Sheffield when the latter was transferred to the Clapham High School in 1898, and in 1917 she again followed Mrs Woodhouse, being appointed Headmistress of Clapham High School. Two years previously she had been elected President of the Incorporated Association of Headmistresses.

Both at Sheffield and at Clapham Miss Escott met with great courage the severe strain which war conditions put upon the schools. The claims upon her wide sympathy increased when she came to London, the rapidly changing conditions of education made serious inroads on her time; but she was never too preoccupied to respond to these calls. She was lately chosen as a member of the Standing Committee of Trust Headmistresses, elected as a medium of communication with the Council of the Girls' Public Day School Trust, and the sane and well balanced judgment, the courtesy and the kindness that she showed in this and other corporate work will be remembered affectionately by her colleagues.

The School has been wonderful, too, in other directions than good fortune in its Heads. "The nursery of headmistresses," of which Miss Paul wrote above, deserves a list to itself. I place in alphabetical order what is, I am told, a complete list of the members of the Staff at the two Clapham Schools who have, so far, become headmistresses of other schools (and, in one instance—that of Miss Paul herself—of Clapham as well), and of University lecturers appointed from the Staff.

PROMOTIONS FROM THE STAFF

HEADMISTRESSES

Miss K. M. Baines	(a) (XXXVIII) Birkenhead
	(b) H.M.I., Woman Staff Inspector
Miss M. M. Berryman	(II) Notting Hill
Miss Bettany	James Allen School
Miss C. Burns	Clifton High School
Miss F. Campbell	Devonport High School
Miss N. Craig	(a) Saltburn High School
	(b) Christ's Hospital
Miss A. H. Davies	Farringtons, Chislehurst
Miss M. E. Fox	(a) County School, Gravesend
	(b) County School, Beckenham
Miss D. Gale	(XXIX) Shrewsbury
Miss F. L. Ghey	St Mary's Hall, Brighton
Miss M. Gilliland	Haberdashers' Aske's School, Acton
Miss E. Glauert	Girls' High School, Scarborough
Miss Grainger Gray	Sandecotes, Dorset
Miss S. Grierson	Uplands, St Leonards-on-Sea.
Miss Heron	Wyggeston, Leicester

Miss Hill	Uplands School
Miss Hockley	Girls' Grammar School, Thame
Miss E. Home	(I) Kensington
Miss M. J. Mowbray	Winchester High School
Miss Page	Skinners' Company's School
Miss A. S. Paul	(a) (II) Notting Hill (b) (XXIV) Clapham
Miss M. Phillp	Stafford High School
Miss Proctor	Surbiton High School
Miss L. Godwin Salt	County School, Bromley
Miss E. Trenerry	The Maynard School, Exeter

LECTURERS

Miss H. V. Abbott	St Gabriel's Training College
Miss C. E. Battye	(a) Goldsmiths' College (b) The Ladies' College, St Leonards-on-Sea
Miss A. H. Davies	Royal Holloway College
Dr W. Delp	Royal Holloway College
Miss A. Kimpster	Univ. Coll. of Wales, Aberystwyth
Miss M. Paine	Goldsmiths' College
Miss A. Russell	Goldsmiths' College
Miss R. Shields	Bedford College
Miss D. Snow	Goldsmiths' College

What the School grew into should now be clearer; what it grew out of must next be told.

The motto "Lampada Tradam"—I will hand on the torch—was very appropriately chosen by and for our first suburban School, opened at Clarence House, Clapham Common, on May 3rd, 1875. Captain Cook had lived in the house—old, Georgian, with panelled rooms, and with three tall lime-trees in front,—and had paced his quarter-deck on its balcony, revolving his adventures in the past. Macaulay was a near neighbour, and Thomas Hood refers to its windows in his *Ode on a Distant Prospect of Clapham Academy*. Snugly housed in these surroundings, the Clapham Middle School, as it was called, won the confidence of various local residents—the Rev. W. Bowyer, the Rector, Lord

PLATE IV

CAPTAIN COOK'S QUARTER-DECK

and Lady Brassey, Dean Bradley, Sir John Gorst—when Miss Mary Alger[1] bore the torch of girls' education into unlit suburban homes. She handed it on in 1877 to Miss O'Connor, first Headmistress (1882–98) of the new Clapham High School, and was succeeded, first by Miss Page (1882–90), and, next and lastly, by Miss Wheeler (1890–98). Meanwhile, in 1894, the Middle School had been remodelled as a Modern School, and in 1898 the Clapham Modern (late Middle) School was closed, and merged in the High School, which was continued after that date as a single foundation under the new, sole Headmistress-ship of Mrs Woodhouse.

What was the difference in type between a Middle (or Modern) and a High School? The Middle Schools were schools with a lower fee—we enjoyed the lease of Clarence House, provided by the generosity of Mr Gassiot, on condition of keeping the fees low—and a comparatively limited curriculum. In Professor Archer's *History of Secondary Education in the Nineteenth Century* we are told that schools of the former class were "deficient in numbers, lacking a clear-cut educational programme, and led nowhere." This description is, perhaps, a little unkind, but the fact that the Clapham Middle School for Girls led the children into the portals of the High School founded seven years afterwards, may be taken as an indication that it led nowhere on its own road. By the same token, it is not necessary to follow in any detail the separate history of our Middle School at Clapham. After all, it really belongs to an old time and to an old type, and no more than a passing tribute need be paid to the work of its successive Headmistresses. But the present writer is fortunate in being

[1] Transferred to our (XIV) Sheffield School in 1877 and to our (XVI) Dulwich School in 1878. Further reference to this distinguished Headmistress is made *s.v.* Dulwich.

able to include a reminiscence of those distant days from the pen of Miss Helena L. Powell, Head of St Mary's College, Lancaster Gate, who was one of its first and most distinguished pupils.

"To this day," she writes, "the scent of limes recalls music lessons in a front room of the school, to one who entered it in January, 1876.

"At that time the idea of public schools for girls was quite new, and we all felt ourselves to be something of adventurers. The school was so very different from those in which our elder sisters had been educated: it was so much more open to ideas from the outer world; had so much more life, and spirit and uplift; we were all so conscious of fellowship, of a corporate aim and purpose and will. Of course we know now that this came from Miss Alger and the staff of like-minded women whom she had gathered around her, through whom she inspired us girls with a sense of the importance of life and of our share in it. At this distance of time my first lesson with Miss Alger stands out clear in my memory. It was a reading lesson, from *Studies in English*, and before setting us to read the passage from *Past and Present* beginning, 'Blessed is he that hath found his work,' she paused to ask what we knew of Carlyle, and by skilful questioning led us to think of him as one of the 'leaders of thought' of the day, and to see what that meant. To be led to think, to judge, to ponder, was a new delight to a girl who had hitherto only 'done lessons'; it was like the first sight of the Pacific to Cortez when he stood 'Silent upon a peak in Darien.'

"Of course the school had none of the 'modern improvements.' It was only an adapted house, with oddly shaped rooms, some much too small for their purpose; there was no central heating and in each room only a few girls could get warm, and only on one side. The Sixth Form, when at last it came into being, had only half the dining room as its abode, and the girls had to clear out quickly to make room for the dining table. But the camaraderie which results from having to put up with inconveniences; the resourcefulness and power of adaptation which are often called out by want of apparatus, went far to outweigh any loss arising from straitened circumstances; and in keenness, and *esprit de corps* the little school in the awkward building has not, I venture to believe, been surpassed by any of the more perfectly equipped schools.

"It is teachers and pupils, not buildings or playing-fields, that make a school, and we had inspiring mistresses, such as Mrs Woodhouse, Miss Luker, Miss Mason, Miss Chambers, and a really remarkable set of girls,—or so it seems to one looking back through all the years. The school had been gladly welcomed at the beginning, by several families of some weight and distinction, then living on the Common, and the Arthurs, Stracheys, Kegan Pauls, Siordets, Paces and Gorsts made a nucleus of girls with a background of cultured homes. Philippa Fawcett was there for a short time, but only as a little girl: the honour of producing a Senior Wrangler must go to the High School."

So we come to the

HIGH SCHOOL

itself, which, as has been noted above, existed concurrently with the Middle or Modern School, from 1882, when Miss O'Connor was moved to it as its first Headmistress. From the very outset of its career, now crowned with exceptional success, the High School at Clapham, with its motto, *Sursum corda*, has taken and maintained a lofty standard of educational and moral aims. Its first home was a large private house known as "The Lawn," on the south side of Clapham Common, where the School has remained throughout its many extensions and expansions. Soon after it was opened, on September 19th, 1882, its numbers necessitated the building of a new assembly hall, which later on served also as gymnasium. Still more space was wanted soon after Mrs Woodhouse became Headmistress in 1898, and the Lower School was moved to "Westbury" situate in Nightingale Lane, where a Kindergarten and Training Department for Students was opened. These small beginnings of nearly a generation ago have, under the continuous direction of Miss L. James, developed into the position which they hold to-day. In the following year, 1899, the land on which the School stood was purchased by the Trust, and in 1900, largely owing to the indefatigable efforts of a Local Committee, the Chairman of which was the late Professor W. H. Hudson, and the Secretary, the Rev. R. Lovett, the present building was erected. Other members of that Committee whose names should be mentioned *honoris causa*, were the Rector of Clapham (the late Canon Greene), Dr Dunbar, the School's medical adviser and constant friend, Mr Haldane, Mr S. Stiff and Mr Sydney Wells. A time of grave inconvenience ensued while the new premises were being built on the old site. Temporary accommodation was found in no fewer than five houses, and Mrs Woodhouse's organizing ability, and, it must be added, her sense of humour, were all necessary to carry the staff and children and parents through that difficult period. The dedication service for the new building was held in January, 1903, and was conducted by Dr Talbot, then Bishop of Rochester, who, with the Hon. Mrs Talbot, was a firm friend of the School; the formal opening ensued in July, 1904, and was presided over by the Duke of Argyll, representing Princess Louise, Patroness of the Trust, who was unfortunately not able to be present.

The enlarged premises gave scope for enlarged activities. Miss E. S. Lees, through many years of long and valued service, developed the School's Science-work in its various branches; in Art, the Training Department for Teachers of Drawing in Secondary Schools under Miss E. Welch was a very remarkable feature, which soon became widely known throughout England; Miss E. Froebel, helped by a large and distinguished staff, was responsible for the Music, and her

influence is described by an old pupil, herself a distinguished musician, as "electric and inspiring." A
system of Medical Inspection, brought by Mrs Woodhouse from Sheffield, and described by her in volume II
of the *Special Reports* issued by Mr (now Sir) Michael
Sadler, when at the Board of Education, was successfully
introduced. This inspection was in the hands of Dr
Dorothea Colman (*née* Caine) and of Miss E. M. Brown,
the chief Gymnastic Mistress, who organised and for
many years ably directed the Physical Training of the
School.

In 1900, two years after Mrs Woodhouse took the
reins, a Secondary Training Department was opened
in connection with the School, under the able lead of
Miss Dingwall. The Teachers' Registration Council,
of which Mrs Woodhouse was a member, representing
the Association of Headmistresses, had recently been
inaugurated, and our Training Department was recognized by the Board of Education. A special reference is due here to the personality of Miss Dingwall
herself, whose position and influence at Clapham were
particularly distinguished. No member of the staff was
more deservedly loved and admired, and her testimonial,
on her retirement, was signed by old pupils all the world
over. The large sum of money which accompanied it
was handed over by its recipient to the Clapham Scholarship Assistance Fund. Among many monuments of
Miss Dingwall's activity is the Clapham High School
Magazine, which she established with great success.
Personally, Miss Dingwall is remembered as a woman
of rare charm and talent.

In 1904, instruction in Domestic Arts was first given
in the School, and, later, a course of training for the
Housewife's Certificate was begun. This was followed
by the institution of a course of training for teachers of

Domestic Subjects in Secondary Schools, which, under the energetic direction of Miss Evelyn Minôt, was steadily developed on more and more useful lines. The Diploma awarded on the completion of the course was endorsed by the Board of Education, and a brilliant future seemed to lie before this branch of the School's activities. With the incidence of war, however, great difficulty arose both in providing adequate materials and in affording a staff paid at the high rates of salary which about this time came into force. These reasons, added to a steady growth of the Lower School and Kindergarten Training Department (immediately following the cessation of the war) which made expansion imperative, brought about the closing, first of the Domestic Teachers' Training Course in 1920 and then in 1921 of the Housewife's Course; and the handing over of Elms House, hitherto reserved for the Domestic Arts, to the Preparatory and First Forms and the Kindergarten students. During the sixteen years that the Domestic Department was in existence, about five hundred Housewives' Certificates were gained, and over one hundred teachers of Domestic Subjects, besides a number of part-time students, had been trained; and it is matter for regret that it had to be sacrificed to the urgent need of economy in salaries and space.

Tribute has been paid above to the Headmistresses who succeeded Mrs Woodhouse after the amalgamation of our Clapham Schools, and to whom the present Head, Miss Barratt, is in all respects a worthy successor. A notable feature of Miss Paul's reign was the opening of an additional studio in June, 1913, by our Patroness, Princess Louise, who was accompanied on that occasion by the late Duke of Argyll. Her reign was further remarkable for its record of University successes, the number of open scholarships won in each year varying from four to nine. Miss Escott's tenure of the Headship will always be memorable, apart from the example of her noble life, for her belief in, and initiation of, the principle of self-government. It is hoped that a tangible memorial to her work in the School will take the form of a new organ.

It only remains to add to this record the list, possibly incomplete, of

BENEFACTIONS

(1) *Scholarship Assistance Fund.*

Established in 1899, it received much support from the Old Girls' Association. The fund has also profited, as noted above, by the gift of Miss J. Dingwall's Testimonial Fund, by a legacy from the late Miss A. E. Escott and the contributions of many other private donors. The money given is used for the benefit of pupils and students who may not be in the running for competition or outside scholarships, but whose work justifies and whose circumstances necessitate some assistance if the pupil or student is to remain at school.

(2) *The Woodhouse Scholarship.*

On her retirement Mrs Woodhouse expressed the wish that the memorial testimonial (subscribed by her many private and public friends) should take the form of a scholarship for the assistance of ex-pupils who are continuing their education. Accordingly, a sum of £20 annually is awarded in alternate years by the Trustees to a student at a University in Great Britain or at some other place of higher education, and to a student in one of the Training Departments connected with the School.

(3) *The Maude Sledge Prize.*

An Annual Prize for Reading given by Lady Foster (*née* Sledge), a former pupil and member of the staff, and awarded by Sir Gregory Foster, Provost of University College, London.

(4) *A History Prize.*

Given, from 1909 to 1920, by Mrs Victor Williams (Miss J. Northcote), a former member of the staff.

(5) *A Mathematical Prize.*

Given by Miss F. Campbell, a former member of the staff.

(6) *A Mathematical Prize.*

Given from 1922 by Miss E. Glauert, a former pupil at Sheffield, and a student and member of the staff at Clapham, for success in Advanced Mathematics in the First Examination.

(7) Valuable gifts have been presented, amongst many others by Mr and Mrs Haldane, silver cups; Prof. W. H. Hudson, oak chair; Mrs Leary, lectern and books; Prof. J. W. Mackail, pictures; Mlle Schwab, the statue of Venus of Milo; not to mention books and pictures greatly appreciated though too numerous to be recorded here.

VI. NOTTINGHAM

The history of our Nottingham High School, the sixth of our foundations, has been one of continuous progress since it was opened on September 14th, 1875, with thirty-four pupils, in a house in Oxford Street. It enjoyed from its start, and even earlier, the keen support and warm sympathy of such important local residents as the Vicar of Nottingham (Canon Morse) and the Head of the Congregational Training College (Dr J. B. Paton). Three daughters of the former and two of the latter were at the School, and Canon Morse, writing to Dr Paton, in a letter dated in 1879, which I am permitted to quote, said: "I have great pleasure in thinking of what we have done together in Nottingham, especially in our High School, which is a priceless boon to the town. So great a boon have I felt it to be to ourselves, that it kept me back from accepting the Subdeanery of Lincoln, which the Bishop offered me."

The first Headmistress was Mrs Bolton, whose name occurred in a former chapter, and will recur in (XVIII) Belvedere (Liverpool) below. On her retire-

ment from Nottingham for private reasons in 1876,
she was succeeded by her Second Mistress, Miss Edith
Hastings—a mode of succession repeated in 1921—
who reigned at Nottingham till 1880, when she was
transferred to our (XXI) Wimbledon School, where the
high tribute notably due to the brilliant qualities of this
Headmistress will be more fitly paid. The succeeding
Headmistresses at Nottingham were: Mrs Luxton, who
was transferred to (X) Brighton in 1883; Miss M. E.
Skeel, who was transferred to (XIII) Maida Vale in
1898; Miss C. C. Clark, who was transferred from
(XX) York, and who retired to everyone's regret in
1921, when her Second Mistress, Miss W. D. Philipps,
M.A., Dublin, was appointed in her stead. At the
time of writing (June, 1923)—and long may it be
true—all these Headmistresses are living, and of all
it may be said that the progress of the School, especially
since 1880, when the Oxford Street house was given
up for the present excellent premises and grounds over-
looking the Arboretum, has been steady and uninter-
rupted. "Through noble aims to noble deeds," is its
chosen motto, and the record has been worthy of the
choice.

At first the scope of the work was somewhat limited
by lack of accommodation. Good results were, however,
obtained, particularly in the Cambridge Higher Local
Examinations, and it is worth noting, that as early as
1876 a society known as The Whetstone of Wit was
started by the elder girls; nine of the members present
at a meeting of the Society held in October, 1922, had
been original pupils of the School. Another feature of
these early days was a somewhat informal, but very
successful, system of training student-teachers in the
School. It may be mentioned, too, that one of Mrs
Bolton's original thirty-four pupils, Miss R. Emily

Russell, is now (1923) a member of the Local Committee of Governors, appointed at Nottingham, as at other schools, in order to meet the Regulations of the Board of Education in connection with Schools in receipt of the Higher Grant. Many Old Nottingham Girls have done, and are doing, excellent work in public life. Two may be selected for special mention. The present Principal of Cheltenham Ladies' College, Miss B. Sparks, was head girl at Nottingham in Miss Skeel's time, and Nottingham, too, had the privilege of training the author of E. Ransome's *School History*. An original member of the staff was Mr Arthur Page, F.R.C.O., Organist of St Mary's Church, Nottingham, who taught singing, with a strong bias towards musical theory, from 1875 to 1912. School songs written by past and present pupils, and set to music by Mr Page, were sung at Commemoration on the twenty-first anniversary of the School in 1896. Mr Page died in London in 1916.

The four years' reign of Miss Hastings left, as was natural in the case of so distinguished a Headmistress, a notable mark on the School. But its chief period of development was during the longer reign of Miss Skeel, which lasted from 1883 to 1898. In 1880, as noted above, the School had moved to its present home in Arboretum Street; the premises were enlarged in 1885, by the addition of an assembly hall, a studio, a laboratory, a music room, a staff room, three class rooms and two cloak rooms. Ten years later again, the numbers had once more outgrown the accommodation, and two more class rooms were added, by raising the roof, and an additional cloak room by utilizing the basement. The lack of playground was supplied in the following year, through the good offices of Sir Joseph Bright, a parent who came to the help of the Council in acquiring a piece of land in Arboretum Street almost opposite the School. Past and present pupils and friends of the School subscribed over £100 towards the cost of laying out this ground, which is still very useful for play and exercises, though no longer adequate to the numbers in the School.

Miss Clark's twenty-three years' tenure of the Head-mistress-ship—peaceful and prosperous years—irradiated by her pleasing personality and by her strong, simple devotion to the highest moral associations connected with educational aims, forms a continuous chapter with the history of Miss Skeel's administration. It is again a story of growing numbers—they had grown to 405 in 1922—and of consequent arrangements for further accommodation. There is also a record of the School's athletic successes, which included the winning of the Hockey Shield, offered by the Midland School Games' Association, for nine years successively, from 1901 to 1909, and again from 1913 to 1915. Three of the four Shields, now in the permanent possession of our Nottingham School, were designed and wrought, in copper mounted on oak, by a former pupil of the School, Norah Stevenson (Mrs Brock), so that in this particular, at least, and we may hope in others, the Nottingham School fulfils the ideal combination of athletics and aesthetics.

It is an office of piety to record one or two names closely connected with this School. Miss Helen Bell, an original pupil in 1875, who died in 1917, is commemorated in a prize for English, which is awarded at the Nottingham Centre of the Oxford Senior Local Examination, and which was founded by her friends in The Whetstone of Wit and Old Girls' Societies. Miss A. E. Fussell, who retired in 1902, after seventeen years' service on the staff as Drawing Mistress, is commemorated in a Fussell Scholarship; Miss Margaret S. McFie, who joined the staff in September, 1914, was decorated with the Order of the White Eagle for her work in Serbia during the War; Winifred Brown, a former pupil, was drowned near Alexandria in a torpedoed vessel in December, 1917, on her way to service in a military hospital, and Miss Edith Pratt, a member of the staff for two years, was awarded the O.B.E. for war service.

Going back to earlier annals, Nottingham had the honour of a visit and speech by Mrs William Grey in 1875, as the result of which the School was founded, and during the first five years of its existence she and Miss Mary Gurney paid several visits to the School. H.R.H. Princess Louise honoured the School with a private visit on December 13th, 1887, and graciously consented to present the prizes in November, 1918, when Her Royal Highness was accompanied by the Duke of Argyll and the Duchess of Portland. The late Dr James Gow, then Headmaster of the Boys' School at Nottingham, and later of Westminster, was a constant friend of our School, and a final line may be given to the kindly interest taken in its early days by Ruskin, who extended to Nottingham the privilege which he extended likewise to several other of our Schools, of lending from his own collection some framed photographs and engravings which were hung on the bare walls of the new class rooms.

PROMOTIONS FROM THE STAFF

HEADMISTRESSES

Miss E. Aitken	High School, Pretoria
Miss C. Ashburner	Lincoln High School
Miss M. G. Beard	(XXXV) East Putney
Miss B. Clay	The Queen's School, Chester
Miss M. Collin	City of Cardiff High School
Miss M. Cromarti	Diocesan Girls' School, Grahamstown

Miss L. HALL	Pontefract High School
Miss HEADLAND	Mussoorie Girls' School
Miss A. HOWARD	(a) Bermondsey Secondary School (b) James Allen School
Miss B. KENNETT	(a) (XV) Ipswich (b) Perse School, Cambridge
Mrs LUXTON	(X) Brighton
Miss OWEN	Girls' School, Grahamstown
Miss PAGE	(a) (V) Clapham (b) Skinners' Company's School
Miss W. D. PHILIPPS	(VI) Nottingham
Miss M. P. POTTER	Plymouth High School
Miss VOKINS	Bolton High School
Miss M. WIGG	Burlington Secondary School

BENEFACTIONS

1885 Terra-cotta plaque representing Athena of Thurium, given by the Old Girls in commemoration of the tenth anniversary of the School.

1900 Fifteen coloured reproductions of frescoes from a Museum in Weimar representing scenes from the Odyssey, and geological specimens for the Museum, given by Miss Chalcraft.

1909 Case of one hundred British Birds collected by the late Dr Percy of Beeston, given by the Misses Percy.

1910 Engraving of Lincoln Cathedral in 1750, given by Miss Mary Gurney.

1918 Oak chair for the Hall platform, given by a few Old Girls of the early days in memory of Helen Bell.

1919 The Fussell Exhibition of £25 a year, founded by Miss Mary Paton in memory of Alice, Annie and Susan Fussell.

1919 The Elizabeth Houston Prize for Classics to be given annually, subscribed for by Old Girls, and a Memorial Tablet in the Hall, given by Miss Clark and the staff, in memory of Elizabeth C. Houston, Classical Mistress, 1905–1918.

1923 Two autograph letters, one written by Elizabeth Fry in 1825 and the other by Florence Nightingale in 1876, given by Miss Paton.

VII. BATH

Motto. "Vincit Veritas."

Our seventh school was opened on September 21st, 1875, in the haunted city of Bath, and the ghosts that walk its terraces may have paused, one thinks, to watch the little deputation of our girls, who marched from Miss Long Fox's boarding-house at 28 Royal Crescent to Mr Frederic Harrison's house at No. 10, in order to bring him a bunch of flowers on his 91st birthday. Some of the ideas for which he fought through the strenuous Victorian days were represented at last in the High School, every Headmistress of which has been inspired in turn by the ideas of gentleness and honour breathed from the grey, old walls rising from the Abbey to the hills.

There have been seven Headmistresses in all:

1875 Miss Susan Wood
1882 Miss Weld (Mrs Griffiths)
1886 Miss Firth (from (XIX) Weymouth)
1895 Miss Heale
1898 Miss Shekleton
1907 Miss Nicol
1919 Miss Fletcher

The twenty-one years, 1898–1919, under Miss Shekleton and Miss Nicol, may be selected as the central years, in which the foundations excellently laid by Miss Wood and her successors were consolidated and extended, and the tradition was handed on which Miss Fletcher is skilfully adapting to the new conditions of wider local government.

Housed in an eighteenth-century building, with lofty rooms and a terraced garden, the School repeated in early years the experience of other schools of the Trust. A Kindergarten was opened in 1877; an adjoining house (No. 6 Portland Place) was taken about ten years

later, and a hall and new class-rooms were provided.
A playing-field and a pavilion marked the occasion of
the School's 21st birthday, and in 1906 No. 4 Portland
Place was added to the two other houses, in order to
provide for growing numbers and widened curriculum.
The next year, Miss Shekleton left for the Redland
High School at Bristol. She had successfully piloted
our school through the changes introduced by the
Education Act of 1902. Bath was one of the first
schools to undergo a "Full Inspection," and the kind-
liness and wise counsel of the late Prof. Withers on the
occasion of that ordeal are still held in grateful remembrance. Miss Shekleton was the first woman member
to be co-opted on the new Bath Education Committee,
and she retained that position, to the great advantage
of her associates, until she left the city.

Miss Nicol was Headmistress from 1907 till just
after the end of the war, and her none too robust health,
ultimately the cause of her resignation, suffered from
the trials of that period. Bath was awarded one of the
German rifles given to schools which had reached a
certain record in War Savings Certificates; and "week
by week," an Old Girl writes, "parcels brought by the
children themselves were despatched to the Central
Agency for prisoners in Germany, and more than one
prisoner, who had the good fortune to be exchanged or
invalided home, came to thank the High School for the
comfort and help he had had from his parcels." This
was not, of course, exceptional to Bath; but the enthusiasm there was bigger than the numbers.

Perhaps we may quote from the same contributor
a testimonial to Miss Nicol herself:

"To write of the school under Miss Nicol is to write the
record of her personality. I think I have never met any one who
was more the centre of her world. She seemed to have the most

perfect and intimate knowledge of all that concerned the working of the school, whether it were the latest requirements of the Board of Education for grants or for advanced work, or the physical well-being of the Staff and the pupils, or the various *minutiae* inevitably connected with the household management of every school. She seemed to know all the children intimately, not only as they appeared in school, but as they were at home— a test of the real teacher. And this knowledge which not once, nor twice, helped her to clear away difficulties and smooth the rough paths that lie before some of us in our critical last years of school life, was not sealed when the girl had left, but from all quarters letters used to come from her Old Girls asking for her advice and her sympathy. One of her staff has said that on entering the school she was impressed at once with its tone— a tone, simple and dignified, which she had experienced in no other school, before or since. Tone or character was the aim of Miss Nicol, rather than mere intellectual achievement, but her girls did well in their various tasks because she taught them it was incumbent upon them to use their talent, to be wise stewards of that which was entrusted to them, whether small or great. To do the duty that lies nearest may be a Victorian adage, but its practice in Georgian days brings an honourable reward. Her rule was firm, severe almost it might seem to an outsider, and she certainly never tolerated the flippant familiarity that so many of the youth of modern times seem to affect, but in any pleasure or in any trouble or sorrow, little ones, as well as their elders, turned instinctively to her for sympathy, and they never turned in vain. She loved to see them happy, and she took the liveliest interest in their games and their sports, but she taught them to find their happiness in working for others."

It should be added, on a more pedagogic note, that, after 1916, the Science teaching at Bath made real strides under Miss Nicol's direct lead.

PROMOTIONS FROM THE STAFF

HEADMISTRESSES

Miss BRUNYATE	Kent College, Folkestone
Miss M. DAVIES	Nuneaton High School

Miss J. A. MACRAE	Calder High School, Liverpool
Miss READ	Derby High School
Miss B. SCHOOLEY	(*a*) Northampton Secondary School (*b*) Now H.M.I. Board of Education

Miss Benton, afterwards Headmistress of our (IX) South Hampstead School, was also at one time Assistant-mistress at Bath, and Miss Philipps, now at (VI) Nottingham, was a former pupil at the same school.

VIII. OXFORD

On November 3rd, 1875, the Oxford High School opened its doors to a little band of twenty-nine girls. It is impossible to listen without emotion when those of the earliest pupils who are still here tell us of the breathless eagerness and the trembling, hopeful anticipation which greeted the first day of the School's life. It began in the Judges' Lodgings, 16 St Giles', under the inspiring Headmistress-ship of Miss Benson, assisted by her successor, Miss Bishop, and by Miss Hitchcock, afterwards Headmistress of (I) Kensington High School. Miss Benson's first message to the School, and it was also her last, will echo and re-echo, as long as the School stands: "Whatsoever things are true, whatsoever things are honest, whatsoever things are just, whatsoever things are pure, whatsoever things are lovely, whatsoever things are of good report—if there be any virtue, and if there be any praise, think on these things." In 1878, the School was moved from the Judges' Lodgings to 38 St Giles', owing to the inconvenience of enforced holidays at the times of the Assizes.

In 1879, Miss Benson retired, and Miss Bishop filled her place. In December of the same year, the first number of the Magazine appeared, and the School

motto "Ad Lucem," and the School flower, the Sun-
flower, were chosen by Miss Bishop. In 1880, the
present School buildings, designed by Sir T. G. Jackson, were opened. In 1884, the Guild of Charity was
formed: its motto is "Disce, doce, dilige," and its
object is best stated in the words of its original founders:
"The principle that must underlie the work is self-
denial for Charity's sake: self-denial in the use of money
and time, in pleasures and luxuries." The staff working
with Miss Bishop included Miss Benton, afterwards
Headmistress at (IX) South Hampstead, Miss F. Gadesden, afterwards Headmistress at (XVII) Blackheath,
Miss Huckwell, afterwards Headmistress at (XVIII)
Liverpool and (XXXV) East Putney, and Miss Ottley,
afterwards Headmistress of the Worcester High School,
since named Alice Ottley School in her honour.

In 1887, Miss Bishop was appointed Principal of
the Royal Holloway College. Her eighteen years'
reign at Oxford had been years of wonderful growth
and development, when the School gratefully responded
to the opportunities offered by the new buildings, and
more gratefully even to the high ideals and the high
standards which the Headmistress and her staff had
placed before it.

Ten full and prosperous years consolidated the foundation of Miss Benson and Miss Bishop under the able
direction of Miss Soulsby, who was equally eloquent
in speech and writing. Her staff included Miss Powell,
whom we met in a former section of this chapter (see
(V) Clapham), and who was to become, successively,
Headmistress of the Leeds High School and Principal
of St Mary's College, Paddington; Miss Faithfull,
afterwards Principal of the Ladies' College, Cheltenham; Miss Mayhew, afterwards Headmistress of our
(X) Brighton School, and Miss Walmsley, afterwards

Headmistress of High Schools at Keighley and at Loughborough.

Miss Soulsby's successor was Miss Leahy, who came from our School at (XXXIV) Dover, and went to our School at (III) Croydon (1902), when the present Headmistress, Miss Haig-Brown, whose very name inspires confidence as an educator, and who had made her mark as an assistant mistress at Blackheath, commenced her distinguished reign.

Turning from the teachers to what they taught, we may note that Miss Leahy's sympathetic attitude towards games accurately gauged the growing desire that girls should share the benefits gained by their brothers from games played in the spirit of comradeship and with healthy enjoyment. Her contribution to the School's life was given generously and freely, but for all too brief a period. In 1903 a Kindergarten and Studio were added to the School buildings. In 1911 a Domestic Economy department was opened at 40 Banbury Road, in order to provide a post-school course for girls over seventeen, but owing to a falling off in numbers during the years of the war, this was closed in 1918. In 1915, a Preparatory branch, for children from four to nine years of age, was opened at Summertown in North Oxford, and in 1920 a similar branch was opened on Boar's Hill. During these years, the number of boarders had been steadily increasing, and by 1920 three boarding-houses were established, at St Frideswides', Bardwell Road; St Bruno's, 41 Banbury Road; and St Hilary's, 332 Banbury Road.

In 1899, the School was honoured by a visit from H.R.H. Princess Louise. In 1921, when Queen Mary accepted an honorary degree from the University, Her Majesty, accompanied by H.R.H. Princess Mary (Viscountess Lascelles), graciously consented to stay for a few minutes outside the School gates, when bouquets were presented by members of the School.

During recent years the School has not been insensible to the universal demand for larger freedom and for fuller opportunities for expression, and has endeavoured, by initiating a limited form of self-government, and by similar movements, to accustom the minds of its pupils to the greater responsibilities and the wider openings offered to the woman of the twentieth century.

PROMOTIONS FROM THE STAFF

HEADMISTRESSES

Miss BAIN	(XXVII) Carlisle
Miss BENTON	(IX) South Hampstead
Miss BISHOP	(*a*) Principal, Royal Holloway College (*b*) Principal, St Gabriel's Training College
Miss BROWNE	Queen Victoria High School, Stockton-on-Tees
Miss CARTER	Preston High School
Miss L. FAITHFULL	(*a*) Principal of Women's Department, King's College (*b*) Ladies' College, Cheltenham
Miss FROST	(XXXIV) Dover
Miss F. GADESDEN	(*a*) Leamington High School (*b*) (XVII) Blackheath
Miss GREY	High School, Durham
Miss HAY	High School, Sunderland
Miss HEWITT	Dunedin High School, New Zealand
Miss A. S. HITCHCOCK	(I) Kensington
Miss D. M. V. HODGE	Lichfield High School
Miss HUCKWELL	(*a*) (XVIII) Liverpool (*b*) (XXXV) East Putney
Miss MAYHEW	(X) Brighton
Miss E. NICOL	(VII) Bath
Miss A. OTTLEY	Worcester High School
Miss H. L. POWELL	(*a*) Leeds High School (*b*) Principal, Cambridge Training College (*c*) Principal, St Mary's College, Lancaster Gate

Miss RUTTY	Burton-on-Trent High School
Miss J. C. THOMAS	Stockton-on-Tees High School
Miss M. WALMSLEY	(a) Grammar School, Keighley
	(b) Loughborough High School
Miss WHITE	Bishop Auckland High School
Miss WOOLLEY	Tottenham High School

IX. SOUTH HAMPSTEAD

South Hampstead was our ninth School, and was opened at a house in Winchester Road, formerly used as a boys' school, under the name of the St John's Wood High School, on March 27th, 1876. The first Headmistress was Miss R. Allen Olney, who rapidly won the support of the important people of the neighbourhood. Dr E. A. Abbott, Headmaster of the City of London School, joined the local Committee; the Vicar of Christchurch, Hampstead, afterwards Bishop of Exeter, sent his daughters to be educated, and the original twenty-seven pupils soon increased to over two hundred. In May, 1882, H.R.H. Princess Louise laid the foundation-stone of the present buildings in Maresfield Gardens, of which Mr Robins, father of one of the original twenty-seven, was, appropriately, the architect. The Princess came again in July, 1897, in celebration of the School's twenty-first birthday, when Lord Spencer, then President of the Trust, was also present. Further extensions have been made to the excellent design of Mr Robins, and in 1920 we were fortunate enough to acquire the next door house in Maresfield Gardens, which had belonged to Sir Ernest Waterlow, and which now houses the younger children.

Miss Allen Olney was succeeded in 1886 by Miss M. S. Benton, who had been in the School as Assistant Mistress (1876–77), and who, after periods of teaching at (VII) Bath, (I) Chelsea and (VIII) Oxford, presided over its destinies for thirty-two years. On her retirement in 1918 Miss D. L. Walker, M.A., Senior Classical Mistress and Sixth Form Mistress at the Leeds High School, was appointed. The clearly defined and consistently pursued policy of Miss Benton during her long reign produced a remarkably steady flow of distinguished successes on both the linguistic and the scientific sides, 115 of the girls taking University degrees, and many of them post-graduate honours. Miss Benton's individuality of view and her power of terse speech made her an influential member of committees of the Headmistresses' Association.

The School has enjoyed the services of many distinguished teachers; perhaps a special word is due to the open lectures on classical subjects given in the early days by Miss Janet Case and Miss E. Sellers (Mrs Arthur Strong). One of its most distinguished classical *alumnae*, Miss Louise Matthaei, who gained a First in Parts I and II of the Classical Tripos in 1903 and 1904, became a Research Fellow and Lecturer at Newnham, and joined the staff of the Council of the League of Nations at Geneva. The Old Girls of South Hampstead stretch to a long list of women workers in almost every department of public life: Mrs Baillie Reynolds (G. M. Robins) in fiction and Mrs Irving (Dorothea Baird) on the stage, are two among many who have spread the School motto of "Mehr Licht."

PROMOTIONS FROM THE STAFF
HEADMISTRESSES

Miss E. Firth	Barrow-in-Furness High School
Miss M. Gardiner	Blackburn High School
Miss E. A. Heppell	North Kensington (Church) High School
Miss A. K. Lewis	(X) Brighton
Miss Macallum	Woolwich (Church) High School
Miss S. Allen Olney	(XVII) Blackheath
Miss M. E. Skeel	(VI) Nottingham
Miss A. Silcox	(XXXVI) East Liverpool
Miss V. Wild	Diocesan Girls' School, Grahamstown

X. BRIGHTON AND HOVE

MOTTO.   "Without the way there is no going.
Without the truth there is no knowing."

Our Brighton School was opened at Milton Hall, Montpelier Road, with seventeen pupils, on June 13th, 1876, after a Public Meeting, held at the Town Hall, and addressed by Mr C. S. Roundell, then Chairman of Council, and Mrs William Grey on the previous Thursday (June 8th). The *Brighton Daily News* of the following day gave a full report of the proceedings, and may still be consulted in the School archives. Four years later, the School was moved to the Temple, and the first public Prize-Giving was held in the Town Hall, Hove, in 1884, when there were about 150 pupils. (In that year, uniquely perhaps, the School possessed, among other societies, a Football Club!) The Temple was one of the buildings of Mr T. R. Kemp (M.P. for Lewes, 1812–16 and 1826–37) famous for Kemp Town, who had built it for use as his own country house. A unique feature was the spiral staircase in the hall, which disappeared in later alterations, and which was alleged, like some others, to have been added because Mr Kemp forgot a stairway in his plans; another is the pilasters of inverted cannon due to memories of what our great-grandfathers called "the war." The School grew in numbers and spread in space—in 1922, it took in the old Vicarage with its excellent grounds—and it has enjoyed the services of a succession of Headmistresses. The full list is as follows:

1. Miss CREAK, B.A. Lond., 1876–83, Newnham College, Cambridge (entered at age of 16), Classical and Mathematical Triposes, held two Headmistress-ships, outside Girls' Public Day School Trust, after leaving Brighton.

2. Mrs LUXTON (*née* BISHOP), 1883–99, for two years previously Head-mistress at (VI) Nottingham.

3. Miss Mayhew (Mrs Head), 1899–1904.
4. Miss Phillimore, B.A. London, 1904–7, for six years previously Headmistress at (XX) York.
5. Miss Lunn (Mrs Doncaster), 1907–17, Cambridge Tripos; transferred to (XIV) Sheffield.
6. Miss Barratt, 1917–21, for three years previously Headmistress at (XXXVI) East Liverpool, now Headmistress at (V) Clapham.
7. Miss A. K. Lewis, M.A. Oxford,

the last and equally excellent of whom, Miss A. K. Lewis, previously Second Mistress at (IX) South Hampstead, was appointed in 1921.

Special mention is due, among Assistant Mistresses, to Miss C. H. Davies, Classical Mistress from 1906 till her death in 1920, and a Brighton Old Girl, in whose memory her friends founded a prize to be awarded each year to the best Classic in the School. Mention is due, too, to the School Guild for work among the poor, which was started in 1886, and which has a fine record of charitable activity. The life and soul of this Guild has been Miss A. C. W. Richards, a member of the staff since 1889, who now acts as the Headmistress's deputy, and whose devoted service is widely appreciated. Other long-service Mistresses, whose valuable work should be recorded, are Miss Anthony (since 1889), Miss Waugh (Art, 1893–1918), Miss Smith-Shand (Sixth Form, since 1905), and Miss Sandell (since 1911), Head of the Preparatory Department.

Another interesting School adjunct is the Library, which contains over 1000 volumes (alas, imperfectly housed), six of which were presented by Ruskin. He had been invited in 1884 to preside at the approaching Speech Day, but neglected to answer the invitation, since he "thought it was only one of the constant requests from mayors and clergymen.... Of course,

I would come thankfully," he added, "if you'd *be* a prize to me—any of you—instead of wanting me to give them to *you*, but I have been twenty years preaching against all competition, and nobody ever minds!" This led to further correspondence, at the close of which Ruskin wrote to the head girl:

Oxford,

My dear Miss Gray,   *Nov.* 20, 1884.

I should hold it a privilege to come and speak to you, if, first, you had read enough of me to know in what sense, and with what convictions I spoke. But is it not unkind to expect an old man to repeat for you what he has written many times, because you like the sensation of being talked to, better than the labour of reading?

I will give you a trial. I order my publisher to send you a list of my published works, let half-a-dozen of you choose each girl a volume for the School Library, and then, reading each one chapter or section of the book she has chosen, depute one, as secretary, to ask me not more than six questions. If they are sensible questions (and not too big ones, as, "How do you think the world was made?" or, "Who is the greatest poet from Homer to Shakespeare?") I'll come and answer them when you meet after the Christmas holidays.

Ever your faithful servant,

J. RUSKIN.

Out of a distinguished list of Old Girls, perhaps the name of Hilda Martindale may be selected. She has held office as H.M. Superintending Inspector of Factories for the Southern Division, and in 1918 was appointed to the O.B.E.

PROMOTIONS FROM THE STAFF

HEADMISTRESSES

Miss BUTLER   Girls' Grammar School, Auckland, New Zealand

Miss CRAIG   {(*a*) Saltburn Girls' Secondary School
{(*b*) Christ's Hospital, Hertford

Miss D. F. P. HILEY (XXXVII) Newcastle
Miss NOLTING Halifax Girls' Secondary School
Miss RYAN
{
(*a*) Bayswater Catholic High School
(*b*) St Thomas, R.C. Secondary School, Durham
(*c*) Now H.M.I.
}

LECTURERS

Miss BONE Bingley Training College
Miss NICHOLSON Maria Grey Training College

XI. GATESHEAD AND
XXXVII. NEWCASTLE

These two Schools, as will appear, were united in 1907, by the absorption into the Newcastle foundation (opened in 1889 as a Preparatory School, and in 1895 as a High School) of the High School opened at Gateshead in 1876.

The three following paragraphs about the combined School are communicated:

Looking back, it may be said that, by its remoteness, the School has suffered, probably more than any other, from a continuous flux of staff. The shortness of tenure is astonishing, when we consider the record in other schools of twenty and thirty years' standing. (There have been six Second Mistresses at Newcastle during the last dozen years.) In these circumstances, we must leave individuals to an indistinguished and yet glorious anonymity. Each has contributed her share to the School's success,—some with all they possessed of mind and heart, and these "lively stones" are built into the fabric.

This transitoriness has no doubt hampered the work of the School, but on the positive side one unforeseen yet natural consequence reveals itself. The inherent character of the School has escaped any particular or personal domination, and persists, not of course uninfluenced, but robustly individual. What is it? There one would expect, and hope, that, as in the case of a living person, each inquiry would receive a different response.

This is only one hazard. There is not perhaps a superabundance of earnestness, or thoroughness, or determination; but there seems to be a large-hearted comradeship, a certain frank and friendly sportsmanship, a sense of justice. And these sterling, fine, upstanding qualities are at times—too rarely, perhaps—relieved, bediamonded, by something even finer—sensitiveness and humour, and the gleam of sympathetic understanding. There is one symbolic act of the School which is the expression, to most of those who love and remember it, of all these outward and inward characteristics, and that is its singing. Not the singing at Prize-Giving, satisfactory in its way and place, but bearing the same relation to the other as a photograph to the living face. The real singing is on breaking-up day, not for anybody else but for themselves naturally and alone, not for impressiveness and show, but for expression and delight. Then the School is most itself and eternal.

Passing now to the separate annals of the two Schools, and starting, chronologically, with

GATESHEAD

the first preliminary meeting to consider the question of founding a School at Gateshead was held in the Committee Room of the Literary and Philosophical Society on August 26th, 1875.

Among the members of the earliest Local Committee were Dr and Mrs R. Spence Watson, names which often recur in the School's history. Miss J. P. Rowden was appointed Headmistress, and Prospect Cottage, Bensham, was rented as the first home of the School, which was opened on September 19th, 1876, with twenty-eight pupils. In August, 1878, a site was purchased on Windmill Hill, where new premises were built and opened on May 8th, 1880, with Miss I. Cooper as Headmistress. A boarding house was started in the same year. In 1881, when the numbers had risen to 200, a gymnasium was opened. In June, 1884, a new assembly room, and in November, 1886, a chemical laboratory and museum were added. In 1889, a Preparatory School was opened in Newcastle under Miss Rendell, succeeded, in 1891, by Miss Hodgson. In 1891 for reasons of health, Miss Cooper resigned her Headmistress-ship, with a regret shared by all who knew and worked with her. The Council gladly acknowledge a great debt to Miss Cooper's work at Gateshead, and later enjoyed the advantage of her services at (XVI) Dulwich and (XXX) Hackney. She was succeeded by Miss Moberly, who was transferred from (XXVI) Tunbridge Wells and who bore a name highly distinguished in the educational world. When it was decided in 1894 to open the Preparatory School at Newcastle as a High School, Miss Moberly was transferred to it, and Miss Vickers succeeded her at Gateshead. In 1897 the twenty-first birthday of Gateshead was celebrated by a great reunion of former mistresses and pupils, a performance of *As You Like It*, by some of the Old Girls, a cantata, a concert, and a pic-nic. In that year a Commemoration Fund was also started, the interest of which was to be added to an already existing scholarship founded in 1894 and tenable at the Newcastle College of Science.

In 1899, on Miss Vickers's resignation, Miss Tooke became Headmistress, and retained that position until the School, in 1907, was merged in the Newcastle High School, to which Miss Moberly was appointed.

The Gateshead School owed much to its Local Committee, of which Dr Spence Watson was for many years the Chairman. In 1888, and, again, in 1902, Princess Louise honoured the School by distributing the prizes. The Old Girls' Guild, formed in 1884, lapsed in 1908, but was revived in 1913, and continues to meet.

NEWCASTLE

The Preparatory School, which had been started in Newcastle in May, 1889, was opened as a High School in January, 1895, with Miss Moberly, transferred from Gateshead, as Headmistress. In a lifetime of less than twenty years, it has taken its secure place as one of the largest and most successful of our foundations. In 1898, the late Albert Earl Grey laid the foundation stone of the present building in Eskdale Terrace, to which the School was moved in May, 1900. In October, 1902, a Royal visit was paid, Princess Louise distributing the prizes at a joint Prize-Giving held with Gateshead. In 1911 Miss Moberly retired after long and distinguished services in Schools of the Trust, and was succeeded as Headmistress by Miss D. F. P. Hiley. Miss Moberly's fine qualities left their mark, but it was only under Miss Hiley that the numbers rose to their present height. In 1917 a separate building for Kindergarten was opened in Eslington Terrace, from which, in 1922, the Kinder-garten classes with two of the Lower Forms were transferred to a house purchased in Jesmond Road.

Like the sister school of Gateshead, Newcastle has made a special point of singing, and it owes much to the long services of Dr Whittaker, who, since his regretted resignation in 1920, has been as assiduous in zeal and kindness as if he were still on the staff. Both the Schools have had many visits from distinguished persons of the neighbourhood; and the services of Mr Alfred Holmes, for many years Chairman of the Local Committee, and of Mr J. J. Gurney, before him, who evinced a keen interest in both Schools, deserve grateful mention.

The School records of 1911 contain an interesting correspondence with Earl Grey, then Governor-General of Canada, about a flag presented by the School to the chief school of "Newcastle on the Miramichi, Northumberland County, N. Brunswick."

BENEFACTIONS

1. The Leblique Memorial Prize is given annually to the best gymnast.
2. There are two Leaving Scholarships usually given to Armstrong College, one of them was inherited from Gateshead, and for this preference is still given to a Gateshead girl.

The "Virgin Mary Hospital" Scholarships tenable at a University, an application of an ancient charitable foundation, are open to Newcastle High School girls as well as to other girls in Newcastle Secondary Schools, and have been gained by High School girls in the years 1916, 1922 and 1923.

The "Mary Gurney School Scholarship," given annually to the best girl out of all the G.P.D. Schools on the First School Examination, was gained by a Newcastle girl in 1922, the three previous awards having gone to Clapham, Bromley and Blackheath respectively.

XII. HIGHBURY

See "Closed Schools" below.

XIII. MAIDA VALE (PADDINGTON)

"Troja fuit"—Maida Vale played a brief but brilliant part, in the very front rank of the leading schools of the Trust, great especially in its classical distinctions. But conditions and circumstances changed, and in 1912 it ceased to be a Trust School, and was taken over by

the London County Council, who needed greatly increased accommodation in that neighbourhood for girls
coming up from their elementary schools.

Its Headmistresses under the Trust were

1877. Miss A. C. ANDREWS.
1899. Miss M. E. SKEEL (*see* (VI) Nottingham).
1907. Miss W. M. SLATER, who was retained in her appointment
after the transfer of the School.

Prominent among those who were instrumental in
starting the School were three Hampstead ladies, Miss
Mary Hart, Miss Ridley and Miss Vernon, who were
helped and encouraged by Canon Duckworth and
others. It was also deeply indebted in its early days to
the special and unfailing kindness of Mrs William
Grey and Miss Shirreff, the former of whom gave
some charming paintings "with her love and sympathy."

The School began its life on March 5th, 1878, with
twenty-seven girls, at Warrington Lodge, from which
it was moved in January, 1886, to very commodious
new buildings erected by the Trust in Elgin Avenue,
which were opened by H.R.H. Princess Louise, and
afterwards received visits, among others, from Mrs
Fawcett, Mrs Garrett Anderson, Sir Joshua Fitch, and
Dr Percival.

The classical tone of those early days was due mainly
to its Headmistress, Miss Andrews, who had strong
views as to the value of the classics: and also, as she
herself testifies, to the admirable teachers who worked
under her, eminent among whom was Miss Janet Case.
Miss Andrews herself, besides her love of Latin, was an
enthusiastic student of French and Italian. Miss Skeel's
Headmistress-ship is remembered for her single-minded
devotion to the truest interests of education, and for the
tact and discretion which she showed in the face of
growing difficulties. Between 1899, when she was
transferred to the School from Nottingham, and 1907

there were various improvements. Gymnastic apparatus was set up in the Assembly Hall, and besides the playground and hard tennis court a field was secured for games. Nature study led to the formation of a Field Club, and in 1902 an orchestra was started. A swimming class was held at the Paddington Baths, and later on the girls took part in matches with the Notting Hill and Kensington Schools.

The Magazine, which was started in very early days, had a strong literary flavour, containing among other things a number of translations from the Greek. Like other schools of the Trust, Maida Vale had an active Old Girls' Association.

In 1907 Miss Slater became Headmistress, and she continued to hold the post until her sudden death in 1914—two years after the London County Council had taken over. Miss Slater, who had been a pupil at (IX) South Hampstead, had taken a First Class in the Classical Tripos, and gained the Gold Medal for Classics at London, thus continuing and enhancing the School tradition. She was a daughter of Mr John Slater, the well-known architect, and a niece of Augustus S. Wilkins, sometime Professor of Latin at Owen's College, Manchester. A tablet, put up by her staff and pupils in the School Hall, commemorates her devotion and enthusiasm.

The staff and pupils have won distinction in many fields. Of direct

PROMOTIONS FROM THE STAFF

HEADMISTRESSES

Miss BEAL	Warrington High School
Miss A. BLAGRAVE	(*a*) Weymouth High School (*b*) Stroud Green High School (*c*) City of London School for Girls

Miss M. E. Brough	Ware Grammar School
Miss Haigh	Reading High School
Miss M. Sunderland-Taylor	Stamford High School
Miss A. Tapson	(IV) Norwich

and among the pupils of Maida Vale have been Miss Ethel Gavin, Headmistress successively of (XXIX) Shrewsbury, (II) Notting Hill and (XXI) Wimbledon; Miss Margaret Alford, a Girton Lecturer, and editor of text-books; Miss Sibyl Frood, Miss Eleanor Phillips and Miss Edith Edwards, Headmistresses respectively of Dudley, Clifton and Fairfield (Manchester) High Schools; Miss Gisela Richter, of the Metropolitan Art Museum, New York; Miss Ethel Abrahams (Mrs Culley), Reid Fellow, and author of *Greek Dress* (Murray); Miss Dorothy Hunt, of Bedford College, and Miss Beatrice Blackwood, Demonstrator of Human Anatomy at the Oxford University Museum. It was not a dead or moribund School, which, perforce of circumstances, we handed over to the Local Authority in 1912.

XIV. SHEFFIELD

Motto. "Help one another to be nobler, purer, more unselfish, braver."

Among provincial schools Sheffield has undoubtedly been one of the most distinguished. It has enjoyed the activities as Headmistress of Mrs Woodhouse (1878–98) and of the late Miss Escott (1898–1917); and, among its first friends and promoters were the Rev. W. Moore Ede, now Dean of Worcester, who presided at the preliminary meeting, Sir Henry and Lady Stephenson, Mrs Wm Smith, Mr and Mrs H. J. Wilson, Mr and Mrs Wycliffe Wilson, Mr J. D. Leader, and Mr and Mrs J. W. Pye Smith.

Shares were taken up locally, Sir H. Stephenson

generously undertaking to meet any deficiency in the number of shares subscribed. Lady Stephenson, among many benefactions, gave the shrubs for the grounds of the new premises in 1884. Just before the opening Mrs William Grey paid a memorable and inspiring visit, the first of several, which did much to attract supporters. The School was opened in March, 1878, in Surrey Street, under Miss Alger, from (V) Clapham, who left, however, in the following July to open our new School at (XVI) Dulwich; and in Surrey Street, in September, 1878, Mrs Woodhouse (see Clapham *supra*) entered on her long and brilliant reign. These first premises rejoiced in a large hall, furnished with a fine organ, where Jenny Lind used to sing, but they were in the heart of the town with no land attached. In 1884, new buildings well provided with art studio, laboratories, gymnasium, tennis court, etc., and attractive in appearance with their mullioned sandstone windows,—soon to be picturesque with creepers,— were opened in Rutland Park, and to them, in 1890, was added a large piece of adjacent land.

The thirty-nine pupils of 1878 had now increased to 350, many coming from the neighbouring towns of Barnsley, Chesterfield, Doncaster and Rotherham. This was made possible by an organized system of private omnibuses, which brought the pupils from the Great Northern and Midland Stations—a distance of two miles—to Rutland Park. But a boarding house soon became a necessity, and for many generations of school girls, Newnham Lodge remained a point of contact between pupils from many parts of the world.

Sheffield and Gateshead were the first schools to introduce gymnastics, which were soon to be a marked feature at Sheffield, where a Swedish teacher was appointed. Medical inspection on entrance was introduced under Dr Helen Wilson, an old pupil, with remedial exercises. In 1879, a Kindergarten was opened, and in the new building soon grew to be a department receiving students for training under a succession of distinguished heads, among whom were Miss Denne, who had studied at Naples under Mme de Portugal, Miss Amy Walmsley, who left to become Head of the Bedford Kindergarten Training College, Miss Edith Chevalier who eventually returned to Cheltenham Ladies' College as Head of the Kindergarten Department, and Miss Macdonald who remained till 1922, seeing with great satisfaction at the end of her twenty years of service the Training Department brought into direct connection with the University. In 1887, by the generosity of Mrs W. Mason Fenn and of her sister Miss Evans, the last "Dame" of Eton fame, the St Peter's Memorial Home for Students, in memory of the Rev. W. Mason Fenn, was started, and it stands for much more in the lives of those to whom it has offered a home than merely the material help which they have found there. In 1907 St Peter's became the University Hostel.

In this short summary it is only possible to say that the character of the curriculum must be inferred from the University and other honours gained.

Exhibits were sent in 1892 to the Chicago Exhibition, gaining the U.S.A. Award and the Chicago Diploma; in 1897 to the Victorian Era Exhibition, when "the exhibits of Sheffield High School were considered by good judges to be the best of the Women's Work Section," and more recently to other similar exhibitions. In 1893 the Association of Headmistresses held their Conference at the School.

Moor Lodge, a large house with a garden adjoining the School, was acquired in 1917, and was added to in

1921, when the Junior School and Preparatory Department and a Chemical Laboratory were accommodated
in those premises. As the School grew in numbers and
attained to a vigorous mental activity, other sides of its
life were developing under the influence of Mrs Woodhouse, who was supported and encouraged by the willing
co-operation of a staff among whom changes were
comparatively rare. Several members of these earliest
pioneers were peculiarly alive to the claims of civic
and social service, among them Miss Helena Maud
Ramsay, Miss L. Phillips, Miss Maude Siordet, Miss
Laurence. In the middle and later periods, two names
must be mentioned, Miss Trotter and Miss Snell, who
have only recently left after more than thirty years of
long and distinguished service to the School; Miss
Snell having earned the gratitude of a long succession
of mathematical scholars, and Miss Trotter, whose
experience included much work as Deputy Head under
successive Headmistresses, having been truly described
as "everybody's friend." No one more conspicuously
expressed the ideal of social service *within* the School
than Miss R. Bragg, who after fifteen years of gifted
mathematical teaching, left to live in Rome with her
sisters, and there continued her kind ministry by wel-
coming successive relays of Sheffield High School
friends, girls and colleagues, sharing with them the
intimate knowledge gained by a twenty years' residence.

Among the School's activities were Reading Circles
and Social Evenings, Drawing and Field Clubs, a
Musical Guild and Choral Society, and during Miss
Lunn's Headmistress-ship in 1918 a Dramatic Society.
Here the School's indebtedness to the Musical Staff
must be recorded—to Mr C. Templeton, Miss Marie
Krause, and especially Miss Elsa Fröbel, who brought
not only the artistic and technical achievement common

to all Madame Schumann's pupils but also the educational principle which she had inherited from her father, Carl Fröbel, the pupil of Frederick Fröbel himself. She realized that no early specialization in music secured those results which attain the highest fruition by being based upon a good general education. Though the treatment was more or less academic and on the lines of professional requirements, the educational and cultured values came first. She loyally accepted Mr John Farmer's régime, securing as it did that wide acquaintance with the best musical literature, and knew that the taste of her pupils built on such a foundation would ring true.

There were from the School's earliest days libraries for school and class rooms, also a museum, and a magazine which the Bishop, Dr Burrows, once declared to be "the best School Magazine he had ever seen," the unique feature, for which readers in many parts of the world were grateful, being the pages devoted to "Distant Friends."

In 1918 the School was divided by Miss Lunn, its third Headmistress, into "Houses," named after Mrs Grey, Miss Gurney, Miss Shirreff and Lady Stanley, and under Miss Aitken a cup is presented annually to be held by "the House which is best in the Year's work," as distinct from games. The Old Girls' Association and Commemoration Gathering early established in the School's history were powerful factors and although during the War festivities naturally died out, yet Miss Aitken's special efforts to link up the generations have been crowned with marked success.

Mrs Woodhouse's practical interest in social work, and her large view of education as bearing on life and not merely in book-learning, supported as she was by a staff which for many years suffered few changes, sowed in successive generations of these pupils the seeds of much helpful and devoted work, such as their support of the H. M. Ramsay Cot in the Children's Hospital, the Ministering Guild and other charities.

These aims were recognized by Dr Quirk, the then Bishop of Sheffield, when he said of his experience as Vicar of Rotherham that many of the leading and most useful women of Rotherham had been Sheffield High School pupils and that they carried into life the noble words on the cover of the School Magazine that "the end of all earthly learning was virtuous action"; and they continued to inspire the School under Miss Escott, who had previously been pupil and Assistant Mistress there, and who, as we saw in a previous section, was later to follow Mrs Woodhouse to (V) Clapham.

The twenty years of Miss Escott's rule (1898–1917) were a time of sustained moral and intellectual achievement. Her work was carried on during a time of great transition in the position of women, a time described by a friend in his memorial sermon as "one of ferment." The Vicar of St Augustine's said, "Miss Escott was the very person gifted by temperament and character to steer a level course through it all. She was open to new ideas. I remember our many conversations on the teaching of the Bible. I imagine that she showed the same desire to move forward with a continuous freedom in dealing with any other subject of teaching. Open to all that was best in the new, Miss Escott was never a doctrinaire nor a fanatic with one idea. She realized that in school she dealt with living material. She completely forgot her own concerns in forwarding those of other people."

She was succeeded by Miss Lunn (Mrs Doncaster) from (X) Brighton, whose marriage took place two years later, and the present Headmistress-ship of Miss

Aitken opened in 1919. The great School is prospering under her rule, and with a confidence inspired by sympathy, and with the view of training girls in responsibility, she has instituted School and Form Committees on which Mistresses and girls work together on many matters of discipline.

PROMOTIONS FROM THE STAFF

Miss Bannister	(*a*) Brighouse High School
	(*b*) St Martin's High School, Charing Cross Road
Miss A. E. Escott	(*a*) (XIV) Sheffield
	(*b*) (XXIV) Clapham
	President, Association Headmistresses, 1915
Miss Gray	Queen's College, Barbados
Miss Heatley	(*a*) Pate Grammar School, Cheltenham
	(*b*) High School, Wolverhampton
Miss M. Hughes	Principal, Training College, Cardiff University
(Mrs Mackenzie)	
Miss Kitchener	Bury High School
Miss L. Phillips	High School, Macclesfield
Miss H. M. Ramsay	High School, Taranaki, New Zealand
Mrs H. Sandford	Queen's School, Chester
Miss F. Tooke	(*a*) (XI) Gateshead
	(*b*) Rutherford College, Newcastle-on-Tyne
Miss A. Walmsley	Bedford Kindergarten Training College
Mrs Woodhouse	(*a*) (XIV) Sheffield
	(*b*) (V) Clapham
	President, Association Headmistresses, 1907

BENEFACTIONS

(1) *Scholarship Assistance Fund.*

Established in the second year of the School through the generosity of local shareholders, who surrendered their dividends for this purpose.

(2) A University Scholarship of £50 for 3 years provided by "Old Girls" and friends during Miss Escott's reign.

(3) An Escott Memorial University Scholarship founded in 1922.

Gifts to the School include portraits of Mrs Woodhouse and Miss Escott, two memorial windows, a swimming challenge shield, two cheques, many Early English reprints and volumes on art, curtains for the hall, a reading desk, casts and statuettes, silver cups, a clock, a gong, book-shelves, many books, pictures and other objects too numerous to mention.

XV. IPSWICH

MOTTO. "Before Honour is Humility."

Our Ipswich School was opened in the Assembly Rooms in Northgate Street, under the Headmistress-ship of Miss Sophie Youngman, on April 29th, 1878. It was a successful school from the start and was remarkable in attracting at a comparatively early date a particular degree of interest in the locality. On May 18th, 1889, H.R.H. Princess Louise visited the School to celebrate its coming of age, and in honour of Miss Youngman's long tenure of the Headmistress-ship. Miss Youngman continued as Headmistress until 1899, and retained till her death, in May, 1907, her connection with, and her interest in, the School. It was largely due to her tact and wisdom and strong personality that public opinion in Ipswich, which was at first a little doubtful as to the venture, became favourable to its prospects, and lent it the support, among other notable local people, of Lord John Hervey, Mr Samuel Alexander, Dr Barrington Chevallier, Dr W. A. Elliston, Mr J. R. Jefferies, Mr R. L. Everett, Mr B. B. Hunter Rodwell, Mr Henry Packard, the Rev. V. V. Granville Smith, Mr Charles Steward, and Mr W. G. Block. Special mention should be made of Lord John Hervey, whose connection and kindly help lasted till his death. The town recognized his work for the School by allocating £50 of the money raised as a memorial to him for a prize to the Ipswich

High School, and called the Lord John Hervey Memorial Prize.

As early as 1894 this local interest was extended by the award of an annual scholarship at our School from the Girls' Endowed School; and when the latter was reorganized and taken over as a Municipal Secondary School in 1906 by the Local Educational Authority, the award was continued. In 1912 a scholarship of £50 a year tenable at a University in the United Kingdom was founded by the municipal authorities, and others have since been added to it. One or more of these (in 1922, two full Scholarships and a smaller one) have been held by pupils of our School since that date. Later, when a Consultative Committee, consisting of representatives of the Local Education Authority, and of local teachers, was set up, the Headmistress and a second member of the staff of the Ipswich High School were elected to serve on it, and they served again on the Area Committee appointed to devise a scheme under the Education Act of 1918. The official draft scheme thus devised recognized that "the School is and will continue to be an important factor in the local system of higher education," and negotiations between the Local Education Authority and our Council in London were set on foot about this date in order to establish closer co-operation between the School and the locality. It was in the autumn of 1921 that, with the appropriate measure of financial help, the High School was definitely placed under the control of a Governing Body consisting of six members of the Authority and five members appointed by the Council of the Trust, the first of whom, it is interesting to observe, was the Hon. Lady Digby, Vice-President of the Trust, and many years Chairman of its Education Committee. Under the Borough scheme of education

M 8

intermediate Borough scholarships for older girls are tenable at the School, and the Borough gives scholarships to the 10 per cent. of elementary scholars admitted, while the County also sends some of its scholarship holders to the School.

The foregoing summary of the administrative history of the School has anticipated the record of its physical growth. Six years after its foundation in Northgate Street, a house adjoining the Assembly Rooms was acquired, and this extension was formally opened by Lady Frederick Cavendish in March, 1890. Fifteen years later again, during the Headmistress-ship of Miss Kennett, who reigned from 1889 to 1909, a sister of the distinguished Cambridge theologian, we purchased a large private house in its own grounds in the Westerfield Road. These buildings were extended and adapted, and were formally opened, in May, 1907, by the Hon. Lady Digby, under the Chairmanship of the late Sir William Bousfield, then Chairman of the Council. Further extensions have been made since. In 1913 a local Trust was created for the purchase of a neighbouring house called Wood View, in order to establish a Domestic Economy Department, and in 1920 the house adjoining Wood View was bought in order to accommodate the whole of the Junior School; meanwhile, a large new laboratory had been added to the main premises, where the transfer of the junior department now made room for a library and a new staff room. The Wood View venture enabled us to start a one-year post-scholastic Domestic Economy course in 1917; an advanced course in Science was recognised, and was followed in 1920 by the recognition of an advanced course in Modern Studies, in which Art and Cookery were included as subsidiary subjects.

Miss Kennett's successor as Headmistress was Miss

Margaret Gale, who again reigned for ten years, when, with her consent, she was transferred by the Trust to our larger School at (XVII) Blackheath, and was succeeded at Ipswich by Miss Ransford, at that time Second Mistress at our (XVIII) Belvedere School, Liverpool.

A few words may, perhaps, be said about the very active students' societies established in connection with the School: a Decorative Club was founded in 1895, for the beautifying of the building, the great majority of the pupils belonged to it, and the School owes to it most of its pictures and busts. The first Ipswich troop of Girl Guides was started by an Old Girl, independently of the School, and consisted almost entirely of High School girls. In 1916, at the express request of many parents, Miss Gale formed a company in the School itself, and shortly afterwards, the first Ipswich troop became a School troop. Miss Gale took a leading part in the movement in the county, and a large number of Girl Guide officers in the town and county are Old High School Girls; a "Brownie" pack was added in 1921. In 1907 a Science Club was started and has held some excellent exhibitions; the School, as noted above, having been particularly successful in its science work.

Miss Youngman arranged the first meeting of Old Girls, who established a scholarship open to pupils in the School between fifteen and seventeen years of age, and tenable for two years. The first award was made in 1897, and the scholarship has been maintained regularly since that date, a small bursary being added to it in 1915, and a second bursary being awarded in 1922. The Association now numbers about 350 Old Girls.

XVI. DULWICH

At Dulwich learning had been cherished as "God's gift" from Elizabethan times. The soil was ready for the seed. Side by side with the new girls' school was Dulwich College, the great day-school to which their brothers went. The High School started on September 17th, 1878, with forty-seven girls. A year later there were 179, and as the numbers continued to increase rapidly, it soon became necessary to extend the buildings. By 1881, when the first public Prize-Giving was held, a large hall, five large class rooms, a music room and additional cloak room space had been added. By 1885 there were over 400 names on the books. In those early days pupils came from Sydenham, Streatham Hill and Norwood, and even from remoter Bromley, Balham, Clapham and Camberwell. But as new schools were built in the neighbourhood, even during the early years, the numbers at Dulwich necessarily declined. This shadow of eclipse deepened perceptibly as years went on, and, in 1913, the difficult decision was reached and carried out, to transfer the School from our Trust to the Church Schools Company. Thus, its history, for the purposes of this record, extends from 1878 to 1913.

In 1895 or 1896 a large field opposite the School was acquired for sports, and not long after two class rooms were thrown together, forming a large and well-equipped laboratory.

Between 1882 and 1892 ten open University scholarships were gained, the total number of University scholarships won by Dulwich girls being twenty, namely: nine at Girton, one at Newnham, one at Bedford College, three at Somerville, five at Holloway, and one St Dunstan's Exhibition.

The School's first Headmistress, and she was by common consent one of the greatest of all the headmistresses who have served the Trust, was Miss Mary Alger, who died at her post in 1894 after a rule of sixteen years. Miss Alger had previous been Headmistress of (V) Clapham Middle School, and then for a few months of (XIV) Sheffield. "Beloved and greatly honoured . . . a true educator, a delightful personality" are words used of her by a colleague, afterwards herself Headmistress of one of the Trust's most distinguished schools. Another writes: "The secret of her influence with girls and staff was her intimate and personal interest in the girls and her knowledge of character. Every week she saw each mistress alone. She had great personal dignity, never-failing courtesy, and a noteworthy tolerance of varying methods, so that her school was distinguished alike by orderliness and freedom." Another lady, who knew Miss Alger both as pupil and as Assistant Mistress, says: "It was such a *comfortable* school, one felt so cared for, so confident of sympathy and of justice." It was left to Miss A. M. Scott, the first Headmistress under the Church Schools Company, to institute a Founder's Day, thus linking up past with present. For the first anniversary gathering in 1910 she asked a few old friends of the School, girls and former mistresses, to write something of their recollections of Miss Alger. These she collected and printed in a small pamphlet, a pious monument, for which old friends of the School may well be grateful to Miss Scott.

We may briefly enumerate the subsequent Headmistresses of Dulwich under the control of the Trust:

Miss COOPER, 1894–1900 (*see* XI and XXX).
Miss L. SILCOX, 1901–8 (*see* XXXVI).
Miss MATTHEWS (Mrs CONNAL), 1909.
Miss FURNESS, 1909–13.

A School Magazine, started under Miss Furness, is still published.

BENEFACTIONS

The "Mary Alger Scholarship" founded by staff and pupils past and present, parents and other friends of the School in memory of Miss Alger.

A Brass Tablet fixed on the "Mary Alger Scholarship" Board was given by the Dulwich High School Association.

Through the efforts of mistresses and pupils the apse in the large Hall was panelled in oak and the names of holders of scholarships inscribed in gold on the panels.

A frieze and scroll inscribed with the School motto "The Utmost for the Highest" were placed above the panelling in memory of Mrs Robinson (Miss Arnold), one of the staff of three mistresses who, under Miss Alger, opened the School in 1878, and of Mrs Rix (Alice Russell), who was first a pupil and afterwards a student mistress.

PROMOTIONS FROM THE STAFF

HEADMISTRESSES AND OTHERS

Miss Arnold	Truro High School
Miss Chambers	(XX) York
Miss D. Knight	Crossley and Porter School, Halifax
Miss M. Parker	Princess Helena College, Ealing
Miss Primrose	(XX) York
Miss A. E. Smith	Carshalton High School
Miss Spiller	Secretary of International Drawing Congress, 1907
Miss Warrell	St Catherine's College, Buenos Ayres

XVII. BLACKHEATH

Blackheath, which was to become one of our greatest schools, was opened on January 7th, 1880, by H.R.H. Princess Louise, who has watched with gracious interest the prosperity which she wished it on that occasion. In 1902, at its coming-of-age, the Princess took tea at the School after distributing the prizes in the Concert Hall, and in 1912 her Royal Highness accepted the invitation to lunch of the Housecraft students, who cooked and served the meal.

One cause of the special honour paid by the Princess to Blackheath in January, 1880, was the fact that it was first of the Trust Schools to be opened in premises built *ad hoc*. No suitable house could be found by the preliminary committee, which had been busy since 1878 with plans for the school, under the lead of the Rev. E. Wilton South, Headmaster of the Blackheath Proprietary School, and of Mrs South, an old Newnhamite. So, the necessary shares having been subscribed, our Council proceeded to build, and Mr E. R. Robson, the architect, was very happily inspired in his task. On a site in a quiet road near the Heath and the Railway-station, he had erected by the end of 1879, a red brick building planned for 300 girls, with possibilities of expansion. It stands in a playground of half an acre, which formerly was fitted with swings, tennis and fives courts, a shady tree with a seat round it, and garden terraces. The front door is approached by a flight of steps, and opens into a wide central vestibule with Headmistress's and Staff rooms on either side, leading into a loggia of five arches, through which there is a view into the Hall below, the main and characteristic feature of the building, lighted from above, with eight class-rooms opening out of it. Two balustraded staircases lead down from the entrance, forming at their intersection, a little rostrum commanding the Hall. At the far end stands the gift of the architect, the figure of Venus de Milo; on the wall above, a cast of part of the Parthenon frieze; on the walls on either side, panels for the Honours lists and between them brackets for classical busts.

The numbers steadily grew under the first Headmistress, Miss Allen Olney, whose sister was then Headmistress at (IX) South Hampstead, till they reached the architect's 300, and in 1882 and twice since he accommodation was enlarged to meet the need.

Miss F. Gadesden, M.A., succeeded Miss Olney in the autumn of 1886, whence we date a brilliant period of thirty-three years' activity, under a Headmistress exceptionally well fitted to guide the destinies, moral and intellectual, of a great girls' school, and to take part at the same time in public work associated with the profession which she adorned. As the curriculum was expanded, the growth of the premises followed suit, and special note may be taken of the record during Miss Gadesden's long reign in University successes, particularly, perhaps, at Girton College; in dancing, games, and gymnastics; in art and homecraft, and in social activities. Pages might be written on these topics, but Miss Gadesden's name belongs to the nation, and will be inscribed in the history of its education. We observed on the first page of the present annals that hers was the voice which was chosen to present an account of the education of girls at the Cambridge Summer Conference in 1900, in a paper which has become authoritative; and for nearly twenty years after that date, including the difficult war-years, Miss Gadesden continued to prove at Blackheath the principles which she laid down at Cambridge. Fortunate in many things, she was fortunate in her successor, when the time came to draw in sail. Her successor was Miss Margaret Gale, then Headmistress of our (XV) Ipswich School, and under her, as under Miss Gadesden, Sir Michael Sadler might well say again, as he said in 1909: "I think of the Blackheath High School as a place where the sun is always shining."

PROMOTIONS FROM THE STAFF
HEADMISTRESSES AND OTHERS

Miss M. Anderson, B.Sc.	Bridgnorth High School (died)
Miss Baldwin, M.A.	Ludlow High School

Miss Dawson	Clapton and Highgate Modern School
Miss Frood, M.A.	Dudley High School
Miss Furniss, M.A.	(XVI) Dulwich Assistant Latin Lecturer, Bedford College
Miss R. M. Haig-Brown, M.A.	(VIII) Oxford
Miss M. A. Howard, M.A.	1. Principal Assistant, London Day Training College 2. County Secondary School, Bermondsey 3. James Allen's Girls' School, Dulwich
Miss Ellen Krabbé	Hereford High School. On Education Committees
Miss Lowe, M.A.	Leeds High School, Member of University Court, Leeds
Miss Major, M.A.	(XXXV) East Putney and King Edward's High School, Birmingham Ex-President Association of Head Mistresses
Miss M. Martin, B.A.	Normanton and Wakefield High Schools
Miss Morant	County Secondary School for Girls, Kentish Town
Miss A. R. Morison	Truro High School and Francis Holland School, Eaton Square
Miss Nimmo	King Edward's Grammar School, Aston, Birmingham
Miss Sanders, M.A.	(XXVI) Tunbridge Wells and (XXXIII) Sydenham
Miss Sheldon, M.A.	(XXXIV) Dover and (XXXIII) Sydenham Member of Borough Council, Lewisham
Miss Siddall, B.A.	Newcastle High School (Church Co.) Head Deaconess, Southwark and Rochester Dioceses
Miss S. M. Smith, M.A.	Sandecotes School, Parkestone (res.) Principal, Hereford Training College
Miss M. Weeks, M.A.	County School for Girls, Richmond, Surrey
Miss Whyte, M.A.	Kettering High School

BENEFACTIONS

1880 From the Architect. Statue of Venus de Milo, Cast of part of Parthenon Frieze and classical busts for Hall.

1894 Old Oak chair and settle from O.G.A.

1899 Mercury from S. I. and M. Weeks.

1902 21st birthday gifts from O.G.A., money invested in G.P.D.S. shares for Library and prizes.

1904 £250 raised by subscriptions and Entertainment towards Playing Field.

1908 Osiander Prize transferred to B.H.S. on closing of Blackheath Proprietary School.

£250 from Fancy Fair invested in G.P.D.S. shares towards expenses of New Wing. Interest to provide 1908 scholarship.

1918 Books from Mr Ingle's Library given by his daughter.

Fifty-two volumes of the *Connoisseur and Art Journal* given by Mrs Francis Dodd, an Old Girl.

1920 Antique Oak Dinner wagon given by Miss Gadesden.

1922 Gift from Miss Rock of nucleus of Natural History Museum.

Two prizes from O.G.A.

From Miss Robson (daughter of the Architect) chair on which Princess Louise sat at Opening.

XVIII. BELVEDERE (LIVERPOOL)

MOTTO. "Sine labe decus."

We went to Liverpool in 1879, where we opened our eighteenth school on March 2nd, 1880. The preliminary negotiations for its foundation had lasted exactly a year. At a meeting held at the house of the Rev. H. I. Johnson, on Saturday, March 18th, 1879, a resolution was passed to take measures for establishing a school in Liverpool at the south end of the town, in connection with the Girls' Public Day School Company, provided 400 shares were subscribed for. During the summer the requisite shares were guaranteed, and at

a meeting held in the following October it was resolved
that a Committee be appointed to make enquiries for
a suitable house. This was found at 17 Belvidere Road,
but there was a technical difficulty in purchasing this
direct for the purpose of its use as a school. Accordingly
Mr William Crosfield very generously came forward
and bought the house in his own name, in order to let
it to the Girls' Public Day School Company, thus
defeating the technical objection. It is pleasant to
remark that Miss Dora Crosfield, a daughter of this
early friend of the School, has been connected with the
Local Committee, among whose members, past and
present, should specially be mentioned Mr Crosfield
himself, Mr and Mrs W. Cropper, Mr and Mrs
Paget, Miss F. B. Melly and Mr H. J. Falk.

The first Headmistress of what was then the Liverpool High School was Mrs Bolton, who, as we have
seen, had been Headmistress of our (VI) Nottingham
School from the date of its foundation until 1876, when
she was obliged to retire for personal reasons. Her
reign at Liverpool lasted from 1880 to 1883, when
she was able to look back to a real degree of success
in the always difficult task of setting a new school at
work. She had begun to build up traditions, she had
introduced a sound system of discipline, based on
Public School methods, and new at that time to the
sisters of Public School boys in the provinces, and she
had the satisfaction, when she resigned in 1883, of
committing her charge to the safe hands of Miss
Huckwell, then her Second Mistress. Old Girls and
new may be interested in the schedule of School Rules,
enforced in Mrs Bolton's day, her own copy of which
is here reproduced. It displays, graphically enough,
the progress effected in forty years:

SCHOOL RULES

1. Pupils may come at 8.45 a.m., but they must behave in an orderly manner till School commences.

2. Each Pupil must be in her place at 9 a.m.

3. Pupils will be reported late if they remain in the house without due cause after 1.10 p.m.

4. No loud talking or screaming allowed in the Dressing-rooms.

5. The DRESSING-ROOMS may be used only for their PROPER purpose. Pupils who remain to take down lessons at 1 p.m. must do so in their own Class-rooms, and Pupils must wait for their sisters in the large Hall, when they are dressed.

6. Pupils are required to change their shoes on coming to School, and also when they go into the Garden for play.

7. Every article used in the School must be marked with the owner's name in full.

8. Monitresses are expected:

   a. To get the Teacher's Mark-books and Class-books ready.

   b. To report rough behaviour during play-time.

   c. To shew the lessons to pupils who have been absent from class.

   d. To bring to the Head-Mistress, before play-time, Copy-books requiring signature.

9. ON THE STAIRS, STRICT SILENCE AND ORDER must be observed AT ALL TIMES.

10. Pupils going from one class to another must remain together and keep strict silence till they are seated.

11. During School-hours no talking above a whisper is allowed among the Pupils, excepting during play-time.

12. Pupils must be perfectly attentive while a class is being taught.

13. Pupils are only allowed to open their desks at specified times.

14. During School-hours each Pupil must keep the books for the morning, that are not in actual use, in a bag under her seat.

15. The Desks must not be displaced.

16. Pupils are required to keep their Desks neat.

17. Each Exercise-book must contain a neat piece of Blotting-paper.

18. No Exercise written in pencil, on loose paper, or in a book without the owner's name, will be accepted by the Teachers.

19. All written work must bear the date of the day for which it is prepared.

20. Exercises will not be accepted unless they are given in at the appointed time.

21. No Exercise will be corrected by the Teacher, unless all faults in the preceding Exercise have been corrected, and the corrections copied out by the Pupil.

22. Every Pupil is required to bring a written excuse if she has been absent, or if her lessons have not been prepared.

23. Pupils attending Afternoon-study are required to work silently from 2.30 p.m. to 4 p.m.

Pupils violating Rules 2, 3, receive a bad mark for unpunctuality.

Pupils violating Rules 4, 5, 6, 7, 10, 11, 13, 14, 15, 16, 17, 18, 19, 20, 23, receive a bad mark for want of order.

Pupils violating Rules 12, 21, receive a bad mark for want of diligence, and are kept in on the following Wednesday, from 1 to 2 p.m.

Pupils violating Rules 9, 22, or behaving in any way disobediently or dishonourably, are reported the same day to the Head-Mistress, and receive a bad mark for conduct.

LIVERPOOL, HIGH SCHOOL FOR GIRLS.

Miss Huckwell, who inherited the School with 208 pupils in attendance, remained as Headmistress till 1893, when the Council transferred her to their School at (XXXV) Putney. Two years later, a scholarship was founded out of funds raised in commemoration of Miss Huckwell's services to Liverpool, and is tenable for three years at a University. Her successor was Miss Cannings, who was transferred to Liverpool from

(XXIX) Shrewsbury and who also reigned for ten years, when she was succeeded, in 1903, by Miss Isabel L. Rhys, M.A., who retained the Headmistress-ship until the end of 1921; her successor, Miss Fraser, M.A., B.Sc., formerly Senior Mathematical Mistress at Cheltenham Ladies' College, has since made a very successful start.

It was during the long tenure of the Headmistress-ship by Miss Rhys that the School became an important unit in the educational system of Liverpool. When she was promoted from an Assistant Mistress-ship to the Head of the School, in September, 1903, the number of pupils had fallen to less than 200, but was doubled before the close of her reign. The School occupied, in the Belvidere Road, only the one house—No. 17—which had been secured in 1879, and now occupies five; and apart from these physical and statistical facts, eloquent though they are of the success which attended her administration, a truer estimate can be formed of what the School owes to her long Head-mistress-ship by quoting one or two extracts from the testimonies rendered to her on her resignation. In the Annual Report of the Council to the Shareholders, we said with complete sincerity that Miss Rhys "courage-ously accepted charge of the School in 1903 at a critical time in its history, and by her success in the face of many difficulties, proved herself one of the ablest Headmistresses who have served the Trust." At her final Prize-Giving on December 17th, 1921, by a series of unfortunate accidents, no member of the Council was able to attend. The present writer had hoped to take the chair, but was prevented at the last moment by illness, and he may, perhaps, quote the following extract from a letter which he sent to the acting chair-man, His Honour Judge Thomas, a firm and constant friend of the School, and which was read aloud on that occasion:

"It was the earnest wish," I wrote, "of every member of the Council that one of us should be present on Saturday night to testify to the extreme sorrow which we all feel at Miss Rhys's retirement from the Headmistress-ship, which she has held, to the immense advantage of our School, for this long period. I can recall, in my personal recollection, more than fifteen years of that period, during which, under three successive Chairmen—the late Sir William Bousfield, the late Prebendary Northcote, and our present good Chairman, Mr Llewelyn Davies—Miss Rhys has always been looked up to as a model of what a Head-mistress should be. The School has prospered under her direction to an almost embarrassing degree. The increase in numbers, involving fresh demands for increased accommodation, has put a very heavy strain upon her own physical strength and organizing power, as well as upon the finances of my Council, restricted as we have been during and since the period of war. We owe her a very big debt for the manner she has reconciled these conflicting claims, and, writing with some knowledge of the facts, I can say with all sincerity that Miss Rhys is bequeathing to her successor, Miss Fraser, for whom I invoke a hearty welcome from the parents, staff, and pupils of the School, a task very considerably facilitated by her own skill, energy, and devotion."

A pleasant feature at that gathering was the presence of Mrs Bolton, the first Headmistress of the School, who, despite her eighty years, came all the way from Hythe in order to attend the Prize-Giving; and among other features on that occasion, to which Miss Rhys referred in her final speech, and which are of even wider interest, were the facts that five of the children who presented flowers to ladies on the platform, were the daughters of Old Girls of the School, and that though the Belvedere School is not a nest of singing birds, yet the words of the songs and of the Ode and of the music of the songs recited, were all composed by pupils of the School.

A few weeks later, in January, 1922, there was a gathering of parents and friends of the School, to say good-bye to Miss Rhys, and to present her with an Address and a cheque in recognition of their deep sense of the great services rendered by her to education during the nineteen years in which she was Headmistress of the School. The speeches and letters of parents of Old Girls, some of which were published in the *Belvedere School Chronicle* of 1921, have been very gratifying to the Council, and testify to the high position held by their School in the great city of Liverpool.

Something of this has been due to the indefatigable work of the School architect, Mr Willink, whose help and advice in local matters, even outside his professional work, has been invaluable for many years past. It may briefly be recorded that our third house in Belvidere Road, No. 15, was opened in January, 1909, and was called the Boarding House until 1914, when it became the School House. After Lancaster—No. 30—on the opposite side of the road, was opened in 1918, as a Senior Boarding House, the School House was reserved for girls under fifteen years of age, which was bought by the Council in 1920. No. 19 was opened as a Junior School in 1912, and served in that capacity till 1918, when the Council bought No. 13 to meet the extended needs of the younger pupils. No. 19 has since served as a Studio. No. 22, known as The Lodge, was opened by Miss Rhys as a Sanatorium early in 1914, but the School has happily been so free from infectious illness that this house has not been taken by the Council. An important collateral result of this extension of our frontage in the Belvidere Road has been a corresponding extension of our rear, and the beautiful gardens at the back of the houses have been fully developed and utilised under the care of Miss Rhys and her staff.

It was in 1911 that the Liverpool High School first became known as the Belvedere School. "The change," writes Miss Rhys, by whose advice it was made, "was forced upon us when the name High School was being used by so many other kinds of schools." I may, perhaps, quote in this place her further remarks on that decision:

"There were about fifty schools," she writes, "in the district called High Schools—some public and some private. We had always called ourselves '*the* High School,' but other schools and people were now getting in the habit of describing us as 'Belvedere High School,' much to our annoyance. There was so much confusion that we finally decided to abandon the name of 'High School' and adopt the distinctive one of 'The Belvedere School.' Three things soon reconciled us to the change: first, the girls found it was far more satisfactory to call 'Play up, Belvedere!' than 'Play up, Liverpool!' at matches and tournaments. Then there seemed to be so many rhymes to the name. (All the School songs in our collection have been written since the change of name.) I think it was Archdeacon Howson's address on 'Belvedere and the Vision Beautiful' (*Chronicle* for 1915) that helped us all to cherish the name as we do now. Every year, of course, adds to the wealth of happy associations with it, and I think the change has been a distinct gain.

FLOREAT BELVEDERE!"

PROMOTIONS FROM THE STAFF

HEADMISTRESSES

Miss BEAUMONT	South Liverpool School
Miss BEVAN	Carlisle and County High School
Miss BLYTH	Oldershaw Secondary School, Wallasey
Miss HEWETSON	{(*a*) (XXXV) East Putney {(*b*) H.M.I.
Miss JARRETT	Ipswich Municipal Secondary School

M

Miss Ransford	(XV) Ipswich
Miss L. Silcox	(a) (XXXVI) East Liverpool (b) (XVI) Dulwich (c) St Felix, Southwold
Miss Wragge	County School, Peterborough

XIX. WEYMOUTH

XX. YORK

See "Closed Schools" below.

XXI. WIMBLEDON

Miss Mary Gurney, who left her Wimbledon home for London in 1879, prepared the way for the starting of a High School in what was then a village, separated from town by miles of open country, and connected with it only by way of Waterloo. On November 9th, 1880, a newly-built private house, 74 Wimbledon Hill, opened its doors to receive twelve girls; the Vicar of Wimbledon, the Rev. Canon Haygarth, read prayers on that first morning. The numbers had grown to 125 when in August, 1887, the fence that divided the garden of 74 The Hill from the field behind was broken through to allow the possessions of the School to be moved to a building erected for it, on land of which the Council had bought the freehold, fronting on the newly-made Mansel Road. A formal opening by H.R.H. Princess Louise had preceded the actual removal. In 1902, 74 The Hill was again taken, this time to house the Preparatory Division; and in 1920 the semi-detached houses, which, with their gardens, fill up the angle between the Main School and the Preparatory, were thrown into one to provide rooms for some junior forms and for music lessons.

Some schools of philosophy maintain that over-population is kept in check by the operation of plague, war and other calamities. Our Wimbledon School defies these experts. Not even the outbreak of fire in war-time interrupted our increase in numbers, dire as were the effects of the calamity which occurred in the early hours of February 17th, 1917. The shock and grief caused by the fire were equalled by the courage, energy and ability with which Miss Gavin, Headmistress, with her staff and the elder girls, salvaged and re-organized; and much practical help was given by friends, notably by the authorities and boys of King's College School. The Council at once took 5 Grosvenor Hill and 14 Ridgway Place to house the Upper and Lower Forms respectively, Miss Jemmett being placed in charge of the latter. War conditions delayed re-building, and it was not till 1920 that the new old School in Mansel Road could be opened, the Duchess of Atholl, an Old Wimbledonian, performing the ceremony on October 27th. The new building in the main keeps the old lines, though it is extended in respect of laboratories, gymnasium, studio, library, dining and cloak rooms. The fire, while sparing the outer walls, had destroyed all inner treasures: the oak bookcases with their contents which were memorials of Emma Mundella and Eleanor Roberts, the lectern given in memory of Alice and Lina Hopkinson, Dr Furnivall's gift of O.E. texts, and Mr and Mrs Hart's of a telescope, the twenty-first birthday clock, pictures, statuettes, furniture and books given by Old Girls and friends; and the Honours' boards. To replace some of these treasures, and to provide the new building with other necessary equipment, a Rebuilding and Equipment Fund was opened, and, thanks to the efforts of past and present girls and of other friends of the School, a two days' sale in July, 1920, realized a sum of £400, the greater part of which has been spent on fittings for the Gavin Memorial Library.

Turning from facts to persons, we come at once to Miss Edith Hastings, the first Headmistress of Wimbledon, who had held the same post at (VI) Nottingham. Miss Hastings, whose brilliant qualities are matched only by her modesty, proved one of the most eminent of many great headmistresses of the Trust, which marked its high appreciation of her value by inviting her, in 1908, to join the Education Committee of its Council, an invitation extended for the first time to one of its ex-headmistresses. After twenty-eight years' zealous work at Wimbledon, Miss Hastings resigned the headship, and from that time till Easter, 1922, was occupied in the inspection of schools, mainly for the Board of Education. The interruption of inspecting during the war made it possible for her to set a fine example of devotion by returning to Wimbledon as a voluntary Assistant Mistress during its time of difficulty, March, 1917, to July, 1918, and this is an appropriate place to record our appreciation of her action. Miss Hastings was a member of the Wimbledon Local Education Authority and of the Consultative Board of the Surrey Education Committee from the time of their formation till she left the High School.

She was succeeded at Wimbledon by Miss Ethel Gavin, M.A. (Girton College, Classical Tripos), who also became a member of the Wimbledon and Surrey Educational bodies named above. Miss Gavin had been Headmistress of the High School at (II) Notting Hill and previously at (XXIX) Shrewsbury. She served on the Council of the Classical Association, and was an influential member of the Executive of the Headmistresses' Association.

During the War she led the School in patriotic efforts, even lending the building twice for use in holiday time as quarters for troops. Her weekly war-talks to the girls will long be remembered. At the time of the fire she was ill; she fought unflinchingly against increasing suffering till the following October, when she was obliged to yield, and, after a painful illness, during which her mind constantly dwelt on the School, she passed away on March 2nd, 1918. Those who knew Miss Gavin in any capacity realized how great a personality had gone. Everyone who worked with her was impressed by her absolute sincerity, complete self-forgetfulness, unfailing generosity of thought and deed, and utter devotion to duty. The many friends who attended the funeral service at St Mary's will not soon forget either the great assembly of girls to whom the Vicar, the Rev. J. Allen Bell, spoke of Miss Gavin's fine example, or the strikingly beautiful reading of the Lesson by the Chairman of the Council, the Rev. the Hon. J. S. Northcote, himself so soon to follow her.

The new Headmistress, Miss Mabel E. Lewis (Newnham College, Classical Tripos), who is so splendidly carrying on the traditions set by her distinguished predecessors, had been Classical Mistress at Wimbledon from 1904 to 1912, and after a year of travel, had been appointed the first Headmistress of the new High School for Girls at Southend-on-Sea. When she returned to Wimbledon as Headmistress in September, 1918, her place at Southend was taken by Miss Swann, the Mistress who had been in charge at Wimbledon during the inter-regnum. Miss Lewis has served on the Council of the Classical Association and, like her predecessors, is a member of the Wimbledon Education Committee.

Among Assistant Mistresses a few must be named

on account of the special character of their contributions to the life of the School. Miss Emma Mundella, in chief charge of the music from the day of opening till her death in February, 1896, gave a great impetus to the musical work by the intellectual quality of her teaching. A voluntary Music Circle for composition and choral singing, lectures, with musical illustrations, by herself, Sir John Stainer, and Sir F. Bridge, the formation of a music library, honours gained in examinations, notably the taking of the A.R.C.M. by a Sixth Form girl aged seventeen (K. Ramsay, afterwards Duchess of Atholl, composer of the music of the School Song), the composition of much music for the use of the School and the arranging of tunes for its *Day School Hymn Book*, all showed the unsparing devotion she gave to her work.

When, in the complete lack of laboratory accommodation, Miss McLeod (afterwards Headmistress of our (XX) York School, and later Mrs Newman) undertook to make of Geology a satisfactory training in Science, her success was remarkable. A good geological collection was quickly formed, Sir Francis Fox and Professor Green of Oxford being among the donors of specimens. Not only did many girls gain distinction in the Higher Certificate examination but one of them, G. Elles, now D.Sc., went to Newnham College with a scholarship, took the "Harkness" Geological Scholarship there, and after gaining a First Class and a Bathurst Scholarship, became Demonstrator to men and women at Cambridge, a post she still holds.

The provision of a laboratory led to the substitution of Chemistry and Physics for Geology, and the appointment of Miss Whiteley (now D.Sc., O.B.E.), who, after admirable work at Wimbledon, left to do research at the College of Science, and had a brilliant career, which properly belongs to the credit of Kensington, the school where she was a pupil.

Miss Nellie Dale, Mistress of the Preparatory Division from 1892 to 1909, worked out in it the Dale method of teaching reading, which has world-wide fame. Not only visitors from distant English-speaking countries but even Poles and Japanese used to come to watch the children, whose independence in their work was as remarkable as the completeness and far-reaching value of the method. Miss Dale lectured for the Education Department and at the Maria Grey and Cambridge Training Colleges and a great number of other places. Not only educational papers but the *Saturday Review* had an article in praise of the method.

Mademoiselle Dussau, who came to England to join the Wimbledon staff, afterwards became governess to Princess Mary, and was with her from nursery age until she was grown up.

An Art Club existed for several years, which had the aims of beautifying the School and of making expeditions to places of artistic interest. Its members once spent a whole day in Westminster Abbey, the Clerk of the Works conducting them even through the Triforium, and the Treasurer of Queen Anne's Bounty hospitably entertaining them. Another noteworthy expedition was at the invitation of Sir Henry Lawrence, Bart., to see the Temple. Miss G. de Lisle, an old Wimbledonian, Art Mistress at the School, who was an active member of the Art Club, maintains its ideals in the School.

The Magazine, started in 1889 will always be associated with the name of Miss Theresa Mundella (Mrs Edwin Hastings), its first promoter. A contemporary of hers, Miss Jemmett, carries on its tradition.

The School motto, *ex humilibus excelsa*, its badge, an

apple, and its colour, apple green, go back to its early days. Of societies, the Wimbledon High School Union, which consists mainly of Old Girls, is the most important. It has from time to time produced "circles," some literary, some practical, and its winter meeting is a social function, largely attended by Old Wimbledonians of every generation.

A scholarship, to be held for one year in the School, is given annually for English literature and composition by Mrs John Hopkinson in memory of her daughter, Lina Evelyn, who lost her life in an Alpine accident together with her sister Alice (also an Old Wimbledonian) and her father and a brother.

The net ball court with its delightful parapet was given by girls past and present, mistresses and friends at the time of Miss Hastings' resignation. The construction was planned and directed by Madeline Agar (landscape gardener to the Metropolitan Public Gardens Association), and the tablet with its inscription and symbolic figures is the work of Helen Rock (sculptor) —two old Wimbledonians who contributed their work as a gift.

The Reference Library in the new building was designed as a memorial of Miss Gavin. The beautiful window and the fireplace and the oak doors were provided out of the gifts made by those who valued the work she had done both in the School and beyond its walls.

The following list of Staff Promotions from the School is as distinguished as any in our records:

HEADMISTRESSES AND OTHERS

Miss J. Archibald	H.M.I. of Secondary Schools
Miss Barratt	(a) (XXXVI) East Liverpool (b) H.M.I. (c) (X) Brighton (d) (V) Clapham

Mlle J. Dussau	{ Governess to Princess Mary during the whole of her education
Miss K. Hurlbatt	Principal of Aberdare Hall, Cardiff University
Miss A. S. Lee	{ (*a*) St Alban's High School (*b*) Kimberley High School
Miss M. E. Lewis	{ (*a*) Southend County High School (*b*) (XXI) Wimbledon
Miss Macdonald (Mrs R. Gray)	{ Examiner in Classics for Northern Universities Kaisar-i-Hind decoration for inspecting places of higher education for girls throughout all India
Miss McLeod (Mrs Newman)	{ (XX) York
Miss Malden	Principal of Hockerill Training College
Miss Masson	{ (*a*) Louth (Lincs.) Grammar School (*b*) Sale County High School
Miss Matthews (Mrs Connal)	{ (*a*) Organizer of Modern Language teaching for West Riding Education Authority (*b*) (XVI) Dulwich
Miss Swann	Southend County High School
Miss Whiteley, D.Sc., O.B.E.	{ Joint Head of the Organic Chemistry Department, Imperial College of Science, South Kensington

XXII. NEWTON ABBOT

See "Closed Schools" below.

XXIII. PORTSMOUTH

On February 21st, 1882, the Portsmouth School was opened in a house in Osborne Road at the corner of Shaftesbury Road, under Miss Ledger as Headmistress. It started with thirty-two pupils, and when, by the end of the year, the numbers had grown to 100, the house next door, known as Burlington House, was added to the original premises. Among its earliest friends and supporters the School gratefully remembers Mr Edmonds, Mr Griffin, Mr Matthews and Canon Grant. The latter was the first Chairman of the Local

Committee, and it was largely through his influence that the support of the Service people in Portsmouth was gained. These have always formed an important element in the School life, though the changes of station inevitable to Navy and Army officers have tended to reduce in this School the average length of the pupils' school-life.

Numbers continued to grow rapidly, and early in 1886 the present convenient and suitable buildings erected by the Trust in Kent Road, Southsea, were opened by H.R.H. Princess Louise. Here, after guiding the fortunes of the School, and inspiring staff and girls alike, for nearly fourteen years, Miss Ledger was compelled by failing health to resign. Her place was filled, in the autumn of 1900, by Miss Adamson, who had previously been at (II) Notting Hill. About this time the Chairman of the Local Committee was Dr Cosmo Lang, then Vicar of Portsea, and since 1908 Archbishop of York, who in May, 1901, gave a farewell address to the girls, on being appointed Bishop of Stepney. The present Chairman of the Local Committee, which, in common with other Schools of the Trust, has recently undertaken increased functions, is the Rev. W. H. David, Vicar of Portsmouth, formerly Headmaster of Kelly College, Tavistock. Features introduced into the School life during Miss Adamson's time were a School Magazine, an annual Harvest Festival, and the Games Club. On November 13th, 1903, on the School's twenty-first birthday, the Princess Louise again showed her interest by distributing the prizes at the Portsmouth Town Hall, which has often been the scene of those pleasant gatherings. The numbers had then reached what proved to be for several years their high-water mark—242. After the war a rapid increase again took place, and the record figure of 350 has been reached.

The year 1905 was a sadly eventful one, owing to the illness and resignation of Miss Adamson. In November of that year Miss Steele was appointed Headmistress, and during her short but particularly happy term of office many "finishing touches" were given to the School life: especially by the annual celebration of the School's birthday—a Founder's Service to which Old Girls are invited; also by a present given annually to the School from the School, and by birthday parties. In September, 1906, a Domestic Science Course for girls over seventeen years of age, was started, and for one year was very successful, but owing to lack of support in the second year, largely due to the provision of a similar very inexpensive course elsewhere in the town, it had to be given up. During the early part of 1908 a beautiful Science room was added to the buildings, the money necessary for this being raised in local subscriptions of shares of the Trust. It was through the efforts of some members of the Local Committee (notably Mr G. W. Edmonds), and the kindness of some parents (notably Dr Cole-Baker) and especially through Miss Steele's own inspiring enthusiasm that the requisite support was gained. Miss Steele, who was transferred in July of the same year to (II) Notting Hill, just before the new room was furnished and in use, had endeared herself alike to the staff, the girls and the town generally in a very remarkable way during her short time at Southsea, and a severe test was put on her successor. The Council were fortunate in securing the services of Miss A. F. Cossey: an Old Girl and a former Assistant Mistress at (III) Croydon, Miss Cossey has proved an ideal supporter of the High School tradition during her long and kindly reign at Portsmouth.

Miss Ledger passed away early in 1908, and in

October of that year the Ledger Memorial Divinity Prize was founded by the Old Girls, and a Commemorative Tablet placed in the Assembly Hall. In 1909 a Reference Library was fitted out from the proceeds of a Sale of Work, the Science Club, now one of the most flourishing of the School societies, was started, and Eastman's Playing Field was rented for use for hockey twice a week. In 1913 hockey was replaced by lacrosse.

In July, 1916, the High School Company of Girl Guides was started, with thirty-one members. In 1919 a beautiful reproduction of the Sistine Madonna was given by the School as a Peace Birthday Thank-offering, and a Service of Thanksgiving was held in the Church of St Thomas on July 16th. In 1920 a new house was taken for the Preparatory Division and was retained till 1923, when the present eminently suitable house facing the Common was bought by the Trust.

Music, art and letters all flourish in our Portsmouth School, which is rather particularly happy in its collection of prints and engravings, many of them gifts from friends. The School song, "Shoulder to Shoulder," was written by an Old Girl, Ada Hatch, and set to music by Mr S. Blagrove, the violin master. But, above all, a word is due to the *genius loci* of Portsmouth, which those who know it love so well for its ineradicable historical associations. Nelson's High Street, crowded with memories, where George Meredith walked as a boy; the Dockyard and Hard, with the Keppel's Head, of Marryat, Kingston and Henty; the birthplace of Dickens in Landport; the Martello Towers in the Solent, recalling our great-grandfathers' war; the new war-memories of yesterday,—it is natural that our Portsmouth girls should grow up straight and true, with England's sea-music in their ears.

PROMOTIONS FROM THE STAFF

HEADMISTRESSES

Miss AULD	Secondary School, Barrow-in-Furness
Miss BUDGEN	Uttoxeter High School
Miss HOWLIN	Palatine School, Blackpool

XXIV. CLAPHAM. *See* (V)

XXV. BROMLEY

MOTTO. "Fides et Opera."

The Bromley School was founded in January, 1883, on the site which it still occupies in Elmfield Road. The hall and three class rooms, with cloak rooms and other minor offices, were later additions, finished in 1887, when the newly-completed building was opened by the Archbishop of Canterbury, Dr Benson. In 1896 the Old Girls' Association was formed, and in 1897 the first number of the School Magazine appeared. In 1903 three new class rooms were added to the buildings, and finally in 1920 The Hawthorns was bought to house the Junior School. The Orchestra has always been a strong point under the able conductorship of Miss Gwynne Kimpton, and in combination with the Sutton orchestra had the honour of playing at the dinner given by the Trust in aid of the Building Fund in 1913. Since 1892 money has been raised for charitable purposes by a Sale of Work, which before the War was held annually, but now is held every two years. Besides subscribing generously to other charities, the School since 1897 has supported the Bromley High School Cot in the Victoria Hospital for Children.

The present Headmistress, Miss Mabel A. Hodge, who belongs to a family many of whom have been honourably associated with education, was appointed to her post in 1908. The School under her has been consistently distinguished by the soundness of its scholarship.

From first to last it has won forty-two Open Scholarships, if the Kent Higher Exhibitions are taken into account. Its most distinguished *alumna*, Miss Dorothy Brock, Litt.D., after a brilliant career at Cambridge, was appointed at an early age to the headship of the Mary Datchelor School, Camberwell, and was one of the two women chosen to serve on the Prime Minister's recent Committee on Classics.

XXVI. TUNBRIDGE WELLS

Motto. "The aim, if reached or not, makes great the life."

Miss Moberly, first Headmistress of the Tunbridge Wells High School, met her twenty-two pupils in a house on Mount Sion, on January 18th, 1883. In 1890, the School had acquired a Sixth Form and a Kindergarten, thus being complete at both ends.

The transference in 1891 of Miss Moberly to (XI) Gateshead opened the long and successful Headmistress-ship of Miss Julian, who reported on the tenth birthday of the School that its numbers had reached 164. The original personnel for two elevens now provided efficient teams for cricket, hockey and lawn-tennis, and Jerningham House was taken for the accommodation of the Upper School. In 1900, a further move was made. A house was secured in Camden Park, which had been used as a preparatory school for boys, and thus required but little alteration. The corrugated iron Assembly Room was moved from Mount Sion, and re-erected as an annexe to the new premises, and in 1902 gymnastic apparatus was put up in it.

The Coming-of-Age of the School was celebrated in June, 1904, and a prize was founded by friends of the School to be given to the girl who was second for the School scholarship.

In 1908 Miss Julian became Principal of the Avery Hill Training College and was succeeded at Tunbridge Wells by Miss Sanders, who, on her transference in 1917 to (XXXIII) Sydenham, was replaced by the present Headmistress, Miss Byrne. In the following year an Advanced Course in Science and Mathematics held jointly with the County School was instituted, and in 1921 a similar Course in Modern Studies began work.

The Old Girls' Association was formed in 1888 and a London branch in 1897. In 1898 the Isthmus Club was started to arrange for matches between present and past girls and staff; and it may be added that the School is equipped with an admirably successful Boarding-house under Miss Molony in succession to Miss Woodcock.

PROMOTIONS FROM THE STAFF

HEADMISTRESSES

Miss D'Auvergne	Secondary School, Welshpool
Miss Kennedy	{(a) Birkenhead Secondary School {(b) H.M.I. Board of Education

XXVII. CARLISLE

See "Closed Schools" below.

XXVIII. SUTTON

Motto. "Fideliter, Fortiter, Feliciter."

On January 17th, 1884, we opened our Sutton School, in Park House, Cheam Road, where Miss Whyte, transferred from (XII) Highbury, met about eighty pupils. Building work had to be begun at once, since there was no house large enough to accommodate them, and in June, 1886, H.R.H. Princess Louise opened the east and west wings of new cloak-rooms, dining-room and hall, five large class-rooms and a studio.

In 1890 Miss Whyte went to live in Scotland, and the Council transferred to Sutton Miss J. F. Duirs, then Headmistress of (XIX) Weymouth, who died abroad in 1903. Miss Duirs had been an Assistant-mistress at (I) Kensington, and was appointed to Weymouth at the age of twenty-eight. Her four years' reign at that school is still recalled with affection and admiration, and the gifts of leadership which she had evinced were proved more fully in her new appointment. It was noted that, on her first day at Sutton, she was able to address each girl by name—a record of thoroughness and application characteristic of her work in the coming years, and due in that instance to her study of the photographs, form by form, which had been presented to Miss Whyte on her retirement. Another notable tradition of her reign is connected with the School orchestra. When this was formed, no one was able or willing to play the double-bass, and Miss Duirs solved the difficulty by giving up some of her scanty leisure in order to learn it herself. The Music at this School is deeply indebted to the labours of Miss G. Kimpton.

Miss Duirs was succeeded in 1903 by her Second Mistress, Miss M. K. Bell, whose twenty years' calm and excellent reign was terminated in 1923 by the transference to Sutton of Miss Lees of (XXXVIII) Birkenhead. Among the more notable events of those twenty years may be mentioned the acquisition in 1911 of a house known as Fernwood, which is used by the Preparatory Department, and the new Wing with two additional class-rooms opened in 1919. It may be noted that a Sutton pupil, Miss M. Howes-Smith, Head-mistress of the Secondary School, Altrincham, had the honour of being appointed History Tutor to H.R.H. Princess Mary Viscountess Lascelles.

PROMOTIONS FROM THE STAFF

HEADMISTRESSES

Miss M. K. BELL	Sutton High School
Miss SANDFORD	Rochester Grammar School

XXIX. SHREWSBURY

Early in 1885 a public meeting was held at Shrews-bury to enlist the sympathy of the townspeople in the establishment of a public school for girls. After much discussion the Girls' Public Day School Company was approached, the chief local advocates of the foundation of a school on broad undenominational lines being Dr Edward Calvert, Miss E. L. Bather, the Rev. Canon Henry Bather, Sir Richard Green Price, Dr Burd, Dr Rope, Dr Eddowes, Major Coldwell and, among other masters of Shrewsbury School, the Rev. G. T. Hall and the Rev. C. J. S. Churchill.

The Council were fortunate in securing, for the first home of the new School, Clive House on College Hill, a beautiful old house, with oak floors, oak-panelled walls and a large garden; and here on May 5th, 1885, the School opened under Miss Cannings, with fifty girls, including nineteen in the Kindergarten. As num-bers increased a large iron building was put up in the garden, and this was opened in the summer of 1886 by the Bishop of Lichfield, Dr Maclagan, afterwards Archbishop of York, who remained always a warm friend of the School.

The popular and successful Preparatory Department,

M   10

which was started at the outset under Miss Rosa Tillyard, and the Kindergarten and Form I, with the
students who came to be trained, were important
elements in the life of the School through its first eight
years. Miss Tillyard was a gifted teacher, of great
personal charm, but to the sorrow of all who knew her
she died in 1888. To perpetuate her memory the girls
and staff of the High School subscribed for a bed in
the Salop Infirmary, together with a beautiful copy of
the Sistine Madonna.

In Music the School was from early days exceptional
in its percentage of pianoforte pupils, due to the
efficient teaching of Mr Hartland, who also took the
Part Singing, and subsequently of Dr Hall, and of Miss
Hume.

Latin was taught in the upper Forms by Dr Calvert,
whose reputation in the town as a scholar and a former
Classical Master at Shrewsbury School added much to
the prestige of the staff.

In July, 1893, Miss Cannings was transferred to our
(XVIII) Liverpool School, and was succeeded by Miss
Gavin.

Owing to the inadequacy of the old premises it soon
became necessary to build a new school. The site
chosen was at the corner of Murivance and Kingsland
Bridge Road, on the line of the old Town Walls. Few,
if any, of our schools can be as fortunate as the High
School of Shrewsbury in their site, or as attractive in
their design. The architect was Mr L. Oswell, and the
School lies on a sunny slope, some hundred yards from
the bank of "Sabrina fair," with the lime tree avenues
of the Quarry, unmatched in England or elsewhere,
close beside it, and, on the heights across the river, the
great school of Sir Philip Sidney and Kennedy and
Charles Darwin. (It is of interest to note that from the

families of members of the staff of that school now come
several of our ablest and most promising pupils.) Further
afield in every direction are the hills which girdle the
Shropshire plain, a country peculiarly rich in interests
historic and scientific, an ideal *alma mater* for girls or
for boys. In these surroundings the new School buildings
were formally opened on January 19th, 1898, by H.R.H.
Princess Louise. The Princess, accompanied by the
Marquis of Lorne and the Duchess of Westminster,
inspected the building, and, after lunching in the dining
room, declared the building open in the presence of the
assembled School and about 500 guests. Her Royal
Highness then distributed the prizes.

In 1900 Miss Gavin, whose ability and high qualities
are dwelt on in connection with (XXI) Wimbledon,
was appointed to (II) Notting Hill. She was succeeded
by Miss Wise, who was transferred to (IV) Norwich
in 1907.

In 1906, on May 18th and 19th, the School celebrated its 21st birthday by a gathering of past and
present pupils. An Old Girls' Dinner, attended also
by various local friends and the former Headmistresses,
Miss Cannings and Miss Gavin, was followed by an
entertainment, also given by the Old Girls.

On May 27th, 1907, the School heard with sorrow
of the death of Dr Calvert, who had been one of the
original shareholders and the constant friend of the
School under three Headmistresses.

In September, 1907, Miss Wise was succeeded by
Miss D. Gale, the present much esteemed Headmistress.

The following note by Miss Gale is here in place:

The opening of new Secondary Schools in the town and
county in 1911 and succeeding years eventually affected the
High School only for good, by arousing a wholesome spirit of

friendly competition both in work and in games. The great War brought its particular obligations, and Old Girls did gallant service for the Red Cross and St John's hospitals in the town and elsewhere. At the School, Emergency Classes in Secretarial Work were started, together with a Secretarial Training Dept., through which 100 students passed in the four years of its existence. Recently two music rooms were thrown into one, and additional cloak-room accommodation provided, so that the School is now able to house comfortably its 260 pupils.

A Boarding House was opened in 1915 by Mrs Stewart Smylie, first on Kingsland, but in January, 1920, further to the south at Cyngfeld, where there is room for forty girls, an ideal site, with its views of the Stretton Hills and the other beautiful hills of south Shropshire.

A member of the Council, himself an Old Salopian, who has had rather special opportunities in the last few years of forming an opinion of the School, writes: "I have been struck by the vigour with which the girls of the Shrewsbury High School express themselves in English, the freshness of their outlook, and the good promise of their work in Greek and Latin. The same energy seems to characterise their games, if one may judge by the championships in summer sports which they have gained year after year among schools of the Midlands. They bid fair to justify the Shropshire boast of 'Proud Salopians'."

It may be added that the "Old Salopian," who writes as above, has founded an Annual Prize of books in the School for an essay in some subject bearing on the British Empire, and that he likewise makes an annual gift to the head girl in the School, to be used by her, from year to year, in any way that she may think, in consultation with other members of the Sixth Form, will be most useful and acceptable. At present, it takes shape as a small Gymnasium Trophy. It is by kindnesses of this kind that the relations between members of the Council and the more distant Schools have been maintained so pleasantly for half a century.

PROMOTIONS FROM THE STAFF

HEADMISTRESSES

Miss ANDERSON (the late)	Bridgnorth High School
Miss B. CARPENTER	Stockton-on-Tees High School
Miss J. FRANKLIN	(*a*) Stroud Secondary School (*b*) Lewisham Grammar School
Miss A. WOODALL	Milton Mount School

XXX. HACKNEY

See "Closed Schools."

XXXI. STREATHAM HILL

MOTTO. "Keep Faith."

Our thirty-first School has known in fuller measure than many another the blessings of a quiet life. The School came into existence as the Brixton Hill High School on February 22nd, 1887, under the Headship of Miss Alice Tovey, one of the many Headmistresses who had gained their early experience under Miss Jones at (II) Notting Hill; her tenure of office came to an untimely end, after a long illness, in 1897. Her successor, Miss Oldham, O.B.E., M.A., had already served the School as Second Mistress; she was therefore no stranger to it when in January, 1898, she was appointed to the post which she held, with unrivalled distinction, till the summer of 1923, when, to the sincere regret of the Council, the parents and the pupils, she decided to retire. To this continuity of tenure is no doubt due the unbroken tradition of ideas and the steady development along certain lines which characterize the School history. It is interesting to trace from an early stage in the School's life a marked, and what was in those distant days, an unusual bias towards the recognition of the individuality of each pupil and the introduction of corresponding differentiation into the curriculum.

At first, however, the School had hard work to obtain a firm foothold in its own neighbourhood. Unlike its "twin" school, (XXXIII) Sydenham, which was opened on the same day, and immediately acquired both numbers and popularity, Streatham Hill began with only seven pupils on its roll, won its way slowly and with difficulty, and was hampered by premises neither convenient nor imposing, as well as by stony local indifference. It took long to convince a neighbourhood of a highly respectable old-fashioned type that a *public* day school was the place in which to educate its daughters, and there was much heart-searching in such crucial matters as the social status of the girls admitted and much dread of a possible "mixture" of social classes. Slowly, however, and after many fluctuations between hope and fear in those who were guiding its infant steps, it became evident that the new School was surmounting its first difficulties and really "making good." In 1894 the numbers had grown sufficiently to justify the erection of a new and handsome building on an excellent site at the top of Streatham Hill. Thither the School removed in the autumn of that year, and the building was formally opened by H.R.H. Princess Louise early in 1895. Its first home still stands shabby and dejected on Brixton Hill, but few are left who recognize it in the humble guise of a furniture depository.

In its new home the School grew and prospered.

In 1900 and 1908 additions were made to the building, while in 1904 a house opposite the School was taken to accommodate the Kindergarten and Transition Classes. Great was the exultation when a fine gymnasium, a library and a second and better laboratory provided it with facilities long craved. Many friends came bearing gifts, and few schools can owe more than Streatham Hill to the thoughtful kindness of its friends and the love of its Old Girls. Love of literature was perhaps the first characteristic it developed, and this is reflected in the size and quality of its store of books. The room set apart for a library and made beautiful by the oak panelling and charming windows, which form a memorial to Miss M. T. Sargant, a beloved mistress in the School's early days, houses the Alice Tovey Library instituted in memory of the first Headmistress, as well as the collection of reference and text-books supplied by the Council. Both have been enriched by countless generous contributions from Old Girls and friends. In the same beautiful room are other presents including, besides pictures and busts, two gifts from the present Headmistress—a fine old oak chest for storage of books and music, and an addition to the oak panelling in the form of an overmantel enclosing Katherine Aldrich's beautiful "Inscription for a Library,"

> Silence within my portals, for I keep
> Watch o'er the mighty who have fallen on sleep.
> Bend down, O living lips, and taste the stream
> Of life eternal, flowing broad and deep.

The lettering on the glass-screened vellum scroll is the work of an artist who is also an Old Girl of the School —and while those words endure upon the library walls many Streatham Hill girls may be helped by them to gain that love of reading which Gibbon said he "would not exchange for the treasures of the Indies."

Interesting too, are the Grace Wilson Memorial Subject-room Libraries, the School's tribute to the long and faithful work of another loved and mourned Assistant Mistress. In the English, Foreign Languages, Mathematics, Science, History and Music rooms are gathered many books bearing on each subject and freely accessible to all who seek there guidance and help in their studies. One of the School's ambitions has always been to establish in its pupils the habit of using books for themselves not only as mines of the information they need but also as companions of their leisure, and this is one of the means it employs to that end.

So constant indeed have been the sympathy and co-operation of parents, friends and Old Girls in the School activities at Streatham Hill that we could almost trace by means of their gifts alone the various interests that have developed there. Music early began to play a prominent part in the School life, and after the splendid gift of an organ for the assembly hall from the first Headmistress, generous offerings followed in succession in the shape of a Bechstein grand piano, a music library, and most modern feature of all, a fine gramophone for the development of the musical appreciation work of the School. Nor has Art, another abiding School interest, lacked generous sympathy. The beautiful modelled and painted frieze in the Assembly Hall, the gift of parents and friends and the work of Mr Matthew Webb, was followed by the statue of the Venus de Milo, presented by the girls in honour of the School's twenty-first birthday in 1908, by the reproduction of the School motto, "Keep Faith," in beaten copper, the gift of the staff, which, framed in dark oak, adorns the entrance hall, and by pictures too numerous to mention by name. Many silver cups, silver and bronze challenge shields for Games, annual prizes for Nature Study, Geography and other subjects have been presented and in some cases founded by parents and friends, and scholarships have been provided for pupils needing aid by the generous kindness of the Old Girls' Association. In such manner are reflected the affection and sympathy with which the School is now regarded in a neighbourhood which at first turned upon it so cold and critical an eye.

The practice of holding Parents' Conferences, timidly initiated before the war, dropped during its continuance, but now firmly re-established, has contributed not a little to a good mutual understanding between School and parents by the opportunities they offer for explanation of School aims and methods and friendly discussion of debatable points.

Other interests followed fast on literature, music and art. Elasticity in curriculum and the discernment of differences of gifts and abilities being a cardinal principle, room was found for a course of liberal secretarial and business training after the age of seventeen. This training was by no means confined to the technical accomplishments, but added to them the study of modern languages, of economics and of the political and social institutions of the modern world. One of the first Advanced Courses in Modern Studies to be established in a Trust School was that which here aimed at directing the thoughts and tastes of elder pupils to the study of economic and social science and therefore gave prominence in its syllabus to the economic side of history and to economic theory. The number of Streatham Hill girls who have passed on to more advanced work at the London School of Economics and have taken their degrees in the Faculty of Economics of the University of London, or who after the Secretarial course have secured hopeful openings in the world of business, has justified what was at the time a new departure in the Schools of the Trust.

Streatham Hill watched and applauded during the war the many-sided activities of its Old Girls, three of whom gained for services rendered to the State the distinction of Officer of the British Empire. The School instituted short courses of secretarial training for the women and girls so urgently called upon to fill the places of men in business and government offices, formed a War Savings' Association which issued certificates to the value of £3000, collected large quantities of clothing and comforts for Belgian refugees and Irish prisoners of war, furnished and equipped the recreation room of the Streatham Red Cross Hospital, provided quantities of comforts for the troops and helped by considerable gifts of money many war charities.

Though Streatham Hill cannot vie with some great Schools of the Trust in the number of its academic honours, it thinks with happiness and pride of its many Old Girls who have attained a measure of distinction in music, letters, art and education, and of others who are active in the public service of the community, and of yet others who have developed in later life powers of initiative and organization now employed in many essential callings and first perceived and encouraged at school. To its system of ordered self-government and its care for individual development the School attributes whatever life and prosperity it enjoys, and it remembers with gratitude the many devoted and gifted women of the assistant staff without whose self-sacrificing efforts on its behalf it could never have attained either happiness or success.

From the foregoing record, which comes, with but minor alterations, from Miss Oldham's own pen, a few lines may be added, on the morrow of her resignation, in recognition of the debt which is due to her twenty-five years' Headmistress-ship. Within and without the School, Miss Oldham has established a record which, in many features, is unique. Beginning her service as Second Mistress under Miss Tovey, in the far-off, early, difficult days, she has lifted our Streatham Hill School right out of the rut of suburban conventionalities on to a height of endeavour and achievement, fully worthy of the public-school tradition which animated the intention of our founders. Carefully, faithfully, and with a rare skill, she has touched the minds of the girls to a sympathy with scholarship and culture; she has humanized their thoughts, and directed their hands to noble deeds. Withal, Miss Oldham has maintained her fresh and vivifying interest in the larger aspects of education. She has taken a prominent part in public life, and in the elevation of the teacher's profession, the dignity of which she has upheld and enhanced. She is a member of the Burnham Committee, a past-president (1917–19) of the Association of Headmistresses, chairman (1922–23) of the London Joint Committee of the Four Secondary Associations, Fellow of the Royal Economic Society, and an Officer of the Order of the British Empire; and, while we repose every confidence in her successor, Miss Gwatkin, whom we appointed in March, 1923, we feel deeply the loss which our roll of Headmistresses has suffered by Miss Oldham's perception that the time has come to take in sail. We may conclude, in the words of *The Times Educational Supplement* of March 3rd, 1923: "This is not the place, nor has the time yet arrived, to place on record all that the Headmistresses' Association owes to Miss Reta Oldham, vice-president and ex-president. But the announcement of her retirement in July from the

Headship of the Streatham Hill High School makes it impossible to refrain from payment of at least a passing tribute of appreciation."

And a last word about the School's poetry. Streatham Hill has been a nest of singing-birds for many years past, and when my colleague, Mr G. H. Hallam, very kindly offered a prize for the best poem on "My School" by a school-girl, he obtained several promising entries from Streatham Hill, of which the following, by a girl aged thirteen, will indicate the excellence of the teaching:

MY SCHOOL

(A DRAMATIC LOOKING-FORWARD)

The Parting of the Ways ("Ave atque Vale."—CATULLUS)

> O rose-red walls, long years have sped
> Since first you sheltered me! I tread
> Once more the well-worn ways, where spread
>   The elm-tree's leafy boughs.
> Though strong the binding ties may seem,
> That link me to my youthful dream,
> Yet must I follow now the stream
>   Of Life's mysterious way.
> I thought with joy this day to greet,
> Yet stand I with reluctant feet,
> Where womanhood and girlhood meet—
>   The parting of the ways.
> And through the coming years I pray
> May all thy training with me stay,
> So that with thankfulness I say
>   "Hail! and farewell!"

A more ambitious response was made—perhaps a little too wide of the Jubilee—by another pupil, Margery Sharp, whose verses were published by Mr Hallam in his "Boys' and Girls' Pages" of the *Victoria League Monthly Notes* (March, 1923), and will also be read here with interest:

THE JUBILEE

EPISODE, 1553. (ROGER PETERS LOQUITUR:)

So, they have killed the queen. Nay, but I know
  She but usurped her passing majesty.
Hath not the Council said it? I am old,
  And meddle not with things too high for me. . . .
'Tis one year and nine months since first I saw
  The Lady Jane, and, since I heard her speak,
Two years. I had been sent to Broadgate House
  With learned books, Italian and Greek,
All fairly bound and wrought; poor maid, she had
  No thought of crowns and tangled policies.

A shaft of sunlight spilt its tawny wine
  Across her book, along the blazoned leaves,
And dripped from off the clasp in amber gouts,
  Besplashing the embroidery of her sleeves—
I caught my breath to hear those wine-drops fall
  And echo in the quiet of the room.
So still she sat, you might have thought her head
  Serene against the arras' purple gloom
Was some poor poet-painter's masterpiece,
  The dear madonna of his grave young dreams.

And she is dead, and all her loveliness,
  The gentle dignity of word and thought,
The quiet learning that amazed the schools,
  The gracious wisdom that no schoolman taught,
All these were crushed between the mills of power:
  All these were lost behind the Traitors' Gate.
Most exquisite and most unhappy maid,
  She has been broken on the wheels of state,
And I may only mourn her silently,
  And guard my tongue against her banished name.

XXXII. SWANSEA

See "Closed Schools."

XXXIII. SYDENHAM

Motto. "Nyle ne drede."

(Wycliff's version of S. John xiv. 1.)

Every year, at the Commemoration Service, past and present girls add to their thanksgiving for "the clearness of vision, the high standard of education and the wise guidance of the first Founders of the G.P.D.S.T.," a second one, "For the foundation of this school in 1887, its growth, and the great inheritance left to us by the first two Headmistresses, Miss Thomas and Miss Sheldon." For it is to these two ladies preeminently that the School owes its character and its success. Their common characteristic—perhaps their only one—a great devotion to the School, has been the source of its success: their difference of outlook and interests have both left a deep mark on the School. To Miss Thomas was largely due its exceptionally rapid growth. On the opening day—February 22nd, 1887—twenty girls (one of them the School's present valued Secretary) were enrolled. In 1889 there were 250 girls. From the beginning the Rev. H. Russell Wakefield, now Bishop of Birmingham, Canon King, and Dr Scott, had shown friendship, but there was an element of strong opposition to the new venture of a public school for girls, and it was by her own remarkable personality and a charm that was almost magnetic, rather than by any outside help, that Miss Thomas was able to overcome all prejudice and suspicion. The growth of the School in efficiency was as rapid as in numbers. In 1891, H.R.H. Princess Louise came to open the Great Hall in the presence of the Marquis of Lorne, Lady Frederick Cavendish, Miss Gurney, Miss Shirreff, Mrs Roundell, Sir Lyon (later Lord)

Playfair, Mr (later Sir) T. Buxton Morrish, and the Hon.
and Rev. E. Carr Glyn, and Lord Aberdare in the Chair.
In 1894 the first University Scholarship was won, at
Lady Margaret Hall, Oxford, by W. Moberly, now
Principal of S. Hilda's College, Oxford.

A house on West Hill, Longton Hall Hotel, built
on the estate of an old Sydenham squire, had been taken
for the School, and one trace of its old use still remains
in a sliding panel window in the Headmistress's room,
once the bar. The School has a long low picturesque
frontage on Longton Grove, and in 1888 the rooms in
this wing were added to the eight in use in the front
part of the house; in 1891, on the old garden behind
them, the present fine Hall, with its gallery, was built.
The year before the Kindergarten, then, as now, an
important part of the School, had been moved into
"Fairlight," a house next to the School, on the other
side of Taylor's Lane. Behind it, in what had been an
old orchard, the new playground was made, with one
asphalt tennis court, laid down in 1896. Hockey was
first played on the field where now the Sydenham
Secondary School stands. A tramcar, neatly fitted up,
was used as a dressing room. In 1899 a large conserva-
tory—the "Winter Garden of Longton Hall"—was converted into a laboratory (now the chemical laboratory);
a studio, opening on to the leads, with a fine view of
Wells Park, had been fitted up ten years earlier at its
south end.

When Miss Thomas retired, in 1901, the foundations of many of the School's most characteristic
activities had been laid—its pre-eminence in modern
languages; its large and flourishing Old Girls' Association; the nucleus of the Orchestra, and the support of the
Cot at the Sydenham Children's Hospital. The School
Magazine dates from 1902.

Miss Thomas was succeeded in 1901 by Miss H. M. Sheldon, M.A. (Mathematical Tripos, Girton College), under whose rule a second period of great activity and development followed.

Physical exercises and gymnastics were thoroughly organized by Miss Wilke, now Head of Chelsea Physical Training College, and Medical Inspection, at present such a feature of the School, was introduced. Games—tennis, hockey, net-ball, rounders—were played, but all, especially tennis, were hampered by lack of space. In order to remedy this handicap Miss Sheldon bought the long lease of a field at three minutes' walk from the School, where two excellent tennis courts were constructed. In five years, by a series of efforts culminating in a Fancy Fair and an Opera, the School paid off the £600, which, with characteristic generosity, Miss Sheldon had lent them free of interest. No school now possesses finer or more convenient courts.

The present convenient system of scoring in the London Schools' Shield matches was devised by Miss Sheldon, and Sydenham held the Tennis Shield in 1899, 1905, 1919 and 1920.

The Orchestra, comprising not only violins, violas, 'celli and double bass, but also flutes, clarinets, bassoon and drum, now became a leading feature of the School's activity, under the able direction of Miss N. Birt[1] with the active co-operation of Miss L. Smith, the chief Piano Mistress. In 1908, to celebrate the School's Coming of Age, £200 were raised by past and present mistresses and girls to found a Music Scholarship.

[1] In 1903 Dr Ernest Walker, of Balliol College, conducted the orchestra, which played a Minuet and Trio, specially composed by him for the School. In 1905 Professor Prout composed a suite for the orchestra, and acted as conductor.

Sydenham was the first of the schools of the G.P.D.S.T. to adopt the division into "houses." The "houses" are named after Foundresses of the Trust— Louise, Gurney, Grey and Stanley. Annual competitions in gymnastics, games and singing, etc., are held, and the School charities, which had their origin in War work are conducted through them. A sum of about £100 a year is now raised by the four houses for charitable purposes—mainly to support the two School Cots at the S.E. Hospital for Children; Lord Roberts' Workshops for Disabled Soldiers, S. Dunstan's Training Home for Blinded Soldiers, the Save the Children Fund, etc.

In 1911 classes in Domestic Economy and Home Arts were opened at 70 and 72 Longton Grove, which are connected with the School by a covered passage, and for our long lease of which the Council are deeply indebted to Miss Sheldon. In 1909 £61. 16s. was raised by an entertainment—Mrs St Loe Strachey's *Masque of Empire* —to convert an old division room into a library. Miss Sheldon gave two oak tables, and many gifts of books from friends and old girls are still received every year. The library now contains, including the art library in the studio and the French and German form libraries, over 1700 books.

In Modern Languages, under Miss Aumas, and later Mrs Delp (German) and Miss Julia Sanders (French and Spanish), the School gained many distinctions. Besides six scholarships for French and German gained at Cambridge, the School three times secured the Gold Medal of the Société Nationale des Professeurs de Français en Angleterre at the Grand Concours, together with the Harrow, Charterhouse, Hachette, Verret and Lefèbre Prizes. Twice the H. Eve Prize for French and German, and the Somerville Prize for Science, open to

M

all the Schools of the Trust, were won by Sydenham girls (E. Bunn, M. Hetley, D. Sparshatt and D. Leverkus), and R. Jacob gained half Mr Hallam's Special Greek Prize. E. Hoffmann took Gold and Bronze Medals for Bookbinding at the Ideal Home Exhibition of 1908, D. Paine the King's Prize for Memory Drawing (R.D.S.). At Girton College F. Wollersen (Florence Buckton) won the prize for English Reading, D. Rappard and D. Fisher the prize for German Reading. L. Blyth a fourth year scholarship and Essay Prize and a Victoria League Essay Prize. H. Deutsch was awarded the Gilchrist Scholarship and Pioneer History Prize. W. Delp a Pfeiffer Research Studentship and the Montefiore Prize; she has since been one of the Examiners for the London University. At the Royal Holloway College, M. Quixley and W. Paine gained Driver Scholarships and M. Paine and K. Bathurst Founder's Scholarships, M. Glennie gained a Chemistry Prize. E. Adams Clark was awarded the Dr Todd Scholarship and Special Prize for Chemistry at the London School of Medicine for Women, and G. Leverkus became in 1922 an Associate of the Royal Institute of British Architects.

In 1917 Miss Sheldon retired, leaving the School with a solid foundation of thorough and of distinguished work, a staff devoted to the traditions of the School, and above all a school whose characteristic spirit was one of happiness, loyalty and freedom. The last of her gifts to the School was a Broadwood grand piano. The School added the inscription

Scholae Dilectissimae
Dono dedit
Helen Maud Sheldon
magistra dilectissima
MCMI—MCMXVII

She was succeeded by the present Headmistress, Miss Adèle Sanders, M.A. (Classical Tripos, Girton Coll.), transferred from (XXVI) Tunbridge Wells, who is admirably extending the fine traditions of the School.

It would be possible to expand these notes into a long catalogue of Old Girls' successes, especially in connection with the War; of benefactions conferred by friends and parents, including most recently the Earl of Birkenhead, who, while Lord Chancellor of England, distributed the prizes in 1921, and gave one in commemoration of his visit; and of promotions from the staff, which have been many and distinguished. But we must be content with a more general statement of the excellent record of the School under its three distinguished Headmistresses. It counts among its past pupils the novelist and playwright who is known as Clemence Dane, and Mrs Starr (Lilian Wade) who was recently awarded the Kaisar-i-Hind medal and bar for the rescue of an English girl from natives in India.

Among Headmistresses appointed from its staff, are Miss Walmsley (Froebel Training College, Bedford), Miss Monk (Blind Girls' School, Chorley Wood), Miss Baker (Grimsby Municipal School), Miss Y. Raymond (Kidderminster High School) and several others. Its former Headmistress, Miss Sheldon, is a member of the Governing Bodies of the Lewisham Grammar School and of the London County Council Secondary Schools at Streatham and at Sydenham. We could not close on a more eloquent expression of the value of our Sydenham High School to the locality.

XXXIV. DOVER

See "Closed Schools."

XXXV. EAST PUTNEY

Motto. "Fortiter et Recte."

It was on September 17th, 1893, that we opened the East Putney High School with fifty-four pupils at Burlington House, Upper Richmond Road, under the Headmistress-ship of Miss Huckwell, transferred to Putney from her successful work at (XVIII) Liverpool. The want of a school in the neighbourhood had been shown by the number of girls who went by train to our (XXI) Wimbledon School, which needed all its space for children from its own district. To a large extent the history of the School, at any rate from the point of view of the Council's Buildings Committee, has been a story of an increasing need of accommodation and of difficulty in securing it. Albert House was added in 1895; Burlington House was given up in 1899, when the Upper School was moved to 18 Carlton Road, where it remained for many years. In 1907 a valuable freehold known as Homefield, on Putney Hill, was obtained and the Junior School was transferred to Homefield a year or two later, the surrounding grounds, which are extensive and attractive, being used by the Senior School for games. In 1914, the twenty-first anniversary of the School, Cromwell Lodge, a commodious house adjoining Homefield, was adapted for school purposes, an Assembly Hall was built and the Homefield's stable and coachhouse were transformed into a studio. The numbers continued to increase during the very difficult years of the War, and in 1918 Lytton House was secured on lease and proved an ideal home for the Junior School. Homefield was again enlarged and room has thus been found or contrived for the 447 girls now representing Miss Huckwell's original fifty-four pupils of thirty years ago.

This constant and rapid expansion has, of course, made serious demands on the organizing ability of the successive Headmistresses of the School, and more than a passing reference is due to the courage, the enthusiasm, and, indeed, the real ingenuity which these ladies have shown in meeting repeatedly the requirements of the neighbourhood, and in the repeated difficulties which those growing requirements have inflicted. Miss Huckwell retained the Headmistress-ship till 1899, when she was succeeded by Miss Major, now Head of King Edward's High School, Birmingham. In 1911 Miss Hewetson, now H.M.I., succeeded, and on her retirement in 1920 the appointment was given to our present valued Headmistress, Miss Beard. A permanent note is struck by the continuous activity of Miss Whiffen, who used to go as a pupil to our Wimbledon School by train, whom her parents sent to our Putney School from the first day of its foundation, and who later became Secretary to its Headmistress; in that capacity she gave devoted and invaluable help to the School work till 1921, when ill-health forced her to retire—we still hope only temporarily.

Special thanks are due to the residents in Putney, whose forbearance and kindness during the many changes in the School premises have been remarkable, and who responded very generously indeed to the appeal for the Building Fund, mentioned in an earlier chapter of this volume, and issued in 1912. To the Local Committee, the Old Girls, and to present parents and friends of the School is due largely the success of our efforts in (1) the purchase of 35 Putney Hill, (2) the building of the assembly hall, (3) the making and equipment of the studio, and (4) the addition of a second asphalt tennis court. Even if we have not been able, chiefly owing to the huge increase in building costs since the war, to do all that we had hoped with our fine site at Putney Hill, yet the grounds acquired have proved extremely useful on the physical side of school life, and we have been especially fortunate at Putney in the provision for games. The Mary Gurney Tennis Court at the back of Homefield was given in 1910 by Miss Mary Gurney, whose name it appropriately bears. It is excellently constructed and, in spite of the fact that it is on clay soil, it has suffered much less from subsidence than the more recent court. A third court was added in 1923.

We may record here the fact that two Old Girls and two members of the staff have proceeded from Putney to Headmistress-ships: Miss F. M. Knipe to the Girls' Secondary School, Boston, Lincs., Miss Mary Huskisson (O. G.) to the Harrow County School for Girls, Miss Beatrice Tonkin (O. G.) to the Abbeydale School, near Sheffield, Miss G. Hugh Jones to the Girls' High School, Constantinople.

XXXVI. EAST LIVERPOOL

See "Closed Schools."

XXXVII. NEWCASTLE: *See* XI

XXXVIII. BIRKENHEAD

The thirty-eighth and last of the Trust Schools was a matter of acquisition, not of foundation. In Village Road, Oxton, there had been since about 1885 a small school variously known as the Oxton or Birkenhead High School, which belonged to a limited company. It was taken over by us in 1901, when we appointed Miss Anderson to be its Headmistress. Unfortunately, her illness and death cut her reign short in 1903, when Miss Baines, now one of H.M. Inspectors, was appointed to Birkenhead from Mrs Woodhouse's staff at Clapham. During the ten or eleven years of her Headmistress-ship, the little transformed school of thirty to forty girls rose in numbers to about 160, and in September, 1905, we quitted the old premises in Village Road and moved to 22 Devonshire Place.

Miss Baines was succeeded by Miss F. H. Johnston, a member of her staff, who was compelled to retire for family reasons after a very brief reign; and there was yet one more change in the Headmistress-ship (Miss Spurling, January, 1916) before the School settled down again in 1917 under the competent guidance of Miss E. M. L. Lees, whom we transferred in 1923 to (XXVIII) Sutton. Her successor at Birkenhead is Miss McCaig.

Apart from these changes in personnel, the progress of the School was retarded for some years by physical causes arising out of the war. It was not till 1918 that the Council were able to relieve the congested class-rooms by taking a lease of 31 Devonshire Place, to which the junior forms were transferred. The pleasant drawing-room of this house has been fitted up as a Chemical Laboratory, which took the place of accom-modation in an attic. In 1920–21, under the almost professional advice of Miss Lees, and with the valued professional services of Mr Willink (see, too (XVIII) Belvedere), a combined gymnasium-hall was con-structed out of the old stable, and the School roll was increased to nearly 280.

An abridged *Comus* was acted by the pupils in 1918, with a resulting contribution of about £45 to the Red

Cross Society; in 1921, Professor Gilbert Murray's *Alcestis* was performed, and produced £21 for the School Library; and in 1922, a Garden Fête in the School grounds raised nearly £300 towards the provision of additional lawn-tennis courts.

CLOSED SCHOOLS

The previous sections of this chapter have dealt with schools of the Trust now in active operation. In the closing section, which follows, a few words are due, by way of record and valediction, to the schools which were also opened with hope of prosperity and success, but which, owing to one or another cause, whether a receding tide of population, or an increase of competition, or to some less analysable conditions in the locality, have had to be closed by the Trust.

As was said in an earlier chapter, the decision to take this final step was never reached without full investigation, and was always postponed till the latest moment compatible with the rights of shareholders and parents, and likewise with the rights of the Headmistress and staff of the School concerned, whose service and power for good were liable gradually to be affected by working in adverse circumstances, and with the consciousness of falling numbers and of failing returns. Looking back from the present safe distance to the tale of these decisions, it may fairly be claimed by the historian that, difficult as they were, they were taken on the whole with sound judgment and discretion, and that in every instance the loyalty and enthusiasm of those more immediately concerned, though stretched sometimes very taut, responded most admirably to the strain.

First in order of foundation of the closed schools was

XII. HIGHBURY AND ISLINGTON

This School was opened on March 5th, 1878, and was closed in 1911. Its first Headmistress was Miss Whyte, whom we transferred in 1884 to (XXVIII) Sutton, and whose successor, Miss Minasi, held the post till the end. These Headmistresses had previously been principals of a girls' school in the district. A Local Committee had been active in preparing the ground for the foundation for some time before 1878, and much gratitude is due, among others, to Miss E. Hickson, Miss E. Pritchard, and Miss L. Sharpe, ladies keenly interested in all branches of social work, who remained in close touch with the School long after it was established. Probably it was due to their sympathy with the broader lines then being opened out to workers for social welfare, that past and present pupils were attracted in such large numbers to the Charity Organization Society, the Invalid Children's Aid Association, and various branches of economic and political activity.

We were fortunate, too, in our premises, as well as in our Headmistresses, and in the type of our pupils. No. 6 Canonbury Place was a picturesque house, a part of which, at any rate, still preserved the original lines and materials of an old Elizabethan manor-house. Formerly the property of the Priory of St Bartholomew, Smithfield, it became in Tudor times a country residence for a Lord Mayor of London, and passed later into the possession of the Marquess of Northampton. As the School grew, the Council acquired the adjacent house and made various additions which yet did not destroy the old-world atmosphere of the building,—an atmosphere which produced a sensible effect upon the minds of all who were accommodated there, apart from the more tangible fact that the water-colour sketches achieved by the pupils of parts of their own school were from year to year among the best productions shown at the Art Exhibitions of the Trust Schools. The Old Girls' Association, which had literary and dramatic branches, besides a club for working girls, is still in existence and keeps in touch with Miss Minasi, who is now living (1923) in Florence, where she pursues her educational interests in connection with the Circolo Filologico and the British Institute of that city.

At least four members of the staff became head-mistresses outside it: (1) Miss Grace Anderson at the County School, Yorks; (2) Miss Cawthorne, at the County School, Bow; (3) Miss Florence Johnson, at the Chichester Training College, and (4) Miss B. Parkinson, at a Diocesan School in India. In the course of fifteen years, thirty-six Highbury girls took University degrees; several of them held scholarships gained at the School in colleges connected with London University, especially Bedford College, and some at Oxford. Helen M. Pixell, B.Sc., was awarded a Reid Travelling Fellowship, to make investigations on marine fauna in Vancouver, and among many other distinguished Old Girls mention may be made of Edith Goodyear, B.Sc., Administrator in Geology and Curator of the Geological Museum at University College, London.

Next in order is

XIX. WEYMOUTH

This was opened in 1880 with only five pupils, and though the number afterwards rose to over one hundred, it was found inevitable in 1894 to close the School for financial reasons. The first Headmistress, Miss Firth, was transferred in 1886 to (VII) Bath, and her successor, Miss Duirs, in 1890 to (XXVIII) Sutton. The last Headmistress at Weymouth, Miss Blagrave, was appointed, after the closure of our School, Headmistress of the City of London School for Girls. An Assistant Mistress, Miss Turner, became Headmistress of the Exeter High School.

XX. YORK

was first opened in November, 1880, as a result of the earlier spade work of Miss Robinson, Miss Wilkinson, Mr de Courcy Baldwin, and Mr and Mrs Gutch, among others, who called a preliminary meeting at the Mansion House in their city. Miss Robinson and Miss Wilkinson, who have long since died, left the deep impress of their personality and of their broad-minded attitude towards women's education on the School and on public life in York. During the period of the School's existence, which lasted till 1907, it performed a really useful function in the city, where the necessity of closing it under the new conditions that then obtained was very much regretted. One of its most successful features was the Kindergarten, established in 1891, largely with the idea of giving the older pupils an opportunity of taking their first year's training as Kindergarten Mistresses in York. Many such students completed their training at the Froebel Institute, and afterwards did good work as heads of Kindergartens and preparatory departments of schools. So successful, indeed, was this branch of our School that it became necessary, in 1904, to provide extra outside accommodation, despite the fact that, already in 1900, the School had been moved from its first premises in Fishergate to a larger and more central building in Petergate, where the science laboratory and an improved gymnasium had been added. Among the seven Headmistresses of the School, two may be specially mentioned: Miss

Clark (1893–98), who was transferred in that year to (VI) Nottingham, where she remained till 1921, and Miss Phillimore (1898–1904), who was transferred to our (X) Brighton School (1904–7), and is now Headmistress of the Girls' Grammar School, Lancaster. Our first Headmistress at York was Miss Chambers (1880–89), and our last Miss Bower (1905–7). Miss M. Ward reigned from 1889–90, and Miss McLeod from 1890–93.

A test of the important place taken by the York High School during the twenty-seven years of its existence is the list of members of its staff and of Old Girls who have filled important posts in later life. Special mention may be made of Miss Clara Ashworth, an Assistant Mistress who has since filled the posts of Head of St Leonard's College and of the County School, Bishop-Auckland; Miss E. M. Berridge, B.Sc., who is now (1923) doing independent research work at the Imperial College of Technology; Miss Foxley, of Manchester University, and Miss Hodsman of the Stockwell Training College.

XXII. NEWTON ABBOT

was opened in 1881, but was carried on by the Trust only for seven years, when, the financial difficulties proving insuperable, it was handed over in 1888 to the then Headmistress, Miss Ridley, who conducted it as a private school of a slightly different type. Its chief importance in our annals is derived from the fact that its first Headmistress was Miss L. Gadesden, whom we transferred in 1884 to (IV) Norwich.

XXVII. CARLISLE

was opened in 1884, after a preliminary meeting at which Dr Goodwin, Bishop of Carlisle, presided. Its three Headmistresses were Miss Bain (1884–92), Miss Beevor (1892–1902), and Miss S. A. Gardiner (1902–9). In 1909, the School was transferred to the Local Education Authority, who converted it into the Carlisle and County High School for Girls. Though its premises were changed at that transference, the County Authorities looked upon the School, not as a new foundation, but as a continuation of the old High School, and have sought successfully to preserve its spirit, tradition and ideals. The Old Girls' Guild, founded by Miss Bain, still counts among its active members Old Girls of the former régime.

XXX. HACKNEY AND CLAPTON

was opened in 1875 and was closed in 1899, owing chiefly to local changes in the population of the district. Its three Headmistresses were Miss Pearse (1875–92), Miss Cooper (1892–94) who came from Gateshead and went to Dulwich, and was thus a little uniquely connected with three schools of the Trust which have either been closed or transferred, and Miss Dawson (1894 till the end).

It was during Miss Cooper's reign that the Hackney School was re-named the Clapton Modern School, and certain changes were made in its scale of fees and in its curriculum, in the hope of adapting the School to the requirements of the neighbourhood. Unfortunately, it was not found possible to maintain it at the level at which the Trust aimed.

XXXII. SWANSEA

was opened in 1888 and closed in 1895, under its first Headmistress, Miss Vinter. It is a school without a history, and the Council need only record that during seven years they sought to spread the ideas of the Trust in the Principality of Wales. The Education Act for Wales, 1899, provided for Intermediate Schools to prepare pupils for the University, and in the success of that legislation the intrusion of our Trust may be forgiven as fully as it has been forgotten.

XXXIV. DOVER

was opened in 1888, in response to an appeal from the town, where the premises had been erected by the efforts of a local company. They found an attractive and a comfortable building capable of holding about one hundred and twenty girls, when Miss Frost, who had been for some years on the staff of our (VIII) Oxford School, first met her forty pupils on September 18th in that year. The numbers rapidly increased, but, owing to the small size of Dover, its lack of easy communication at that date with neighbouring places, and the shifting population of a garrison-town, which has always been felt so much at (XXIII) Portsmouth, it proved impossible to bring the numbers up to an average high enough to make the School financially successful. Educationally, it did splendid work, and some of its Old Girls who went on to the Universities have since held important posts. Miss Frost had to resign her post in 1895, owing to failing health, and died shortly afterwards. Her successor, Miss Leahy, who had been an Assistant Mistress in the School, and who had left it to become Headmistress of the Girls' High School in Jersey, only remained at Dover from

1895 to 1898, when we transferred her as Head-mistress to (VIII) Oxford, and subsequently to (III) Croydon. Her successor at Dover was Miss Sheldon, whom we again kept there only for three years, trans-ferring her in 1901 to (XXXIII) Sydenham, and the last Headmistress of our Dover School was Miss Courteney, who had been an Assistant Mistress at Sydenham. We closed the School in 1908.

In looking back, it is, perhaps, possible that the rather rapid changes in the Headmistress-ship may have militated against success. The difficulty was, how-ever, that with women of the calibre of Miss Leahy and Miss Sheldon, it was hardly possible, and certainly would not have been right, to keep them in a small school constantly struggling against financial conditions, when their powers and talents were available for larger and growing establishments. Probably the truer re-flection is that Dover was fortunate, during its existence as a Trust School, in enjoying during six consecutive years, the services of two such brilliant Headmistresses.

XXXVI. EAST LIVERPOOL

The last school in this group was opened as recently as 1891 in a large house with beautiful rooms over-looking Newsham Park. Its first Headmistress, Miss Lucy Silcox, was transferrred in 1900 to (XVI) Dul-wich, and is now Headmistress of St Felix School, Southwold. Her sister, Miss A. Silcox, who succeeded her, left East Liverpool in 1909 to become Head-mistress of the Thoresby School, and is now Dean of the Women Students at Leeds University. The third and last Headmistress at East Liverpool was Miss Barratt, in whose reign the School was closed in 1912, and who afterwards became Headmistress, successively, of our (X) Brighton and (V) Clapham Schools, at the latter of which she still reigns. The cause of the closing of East Liverpool was the municipal provision for secondary education in the neighbourhood. It was eminently successful in training post-graduate students in connection with the local university. Several of its Assistant Mistresses became heads of other schools: Miss Clay at the Queen's School, Chester; Miss Parker at the Princess Helena College, Ealing; Miss Boys at St Margaret's, Bushey; Miss Christopher at the Durham Training College; Miss Loveday at St Catherine's School, Fifeshire; and Miss Rowell at St Peter's College, Peterborough. Two of its Old Girls also became heads of secondary schools, Miss C. Williams at Faversham, and Miss F. Henry at Spalding. It was a school which enjoyed, during its flourishing-time, the interest of many distinguished visitors, among others our patroness, H.R.H. Princess Louise, the late Countess of Derby, Lady Frederick Cavendish, Sir Oliver Lodge, and the late Professor Sir Walter Raleigh, who gave several lectures at the School.

It may be added, in order to complete this sectional history of our Schools, that we have been approached, even in quite recent times, with requests to found or take over schools in various districts, but that our enterprise in that direction is now at an end.

CHAPTER V

THE SCHOOLS AND THE STATE

NOBODY, and, still less, no multiple body, can live a crowded existence for fifty years without (1) coming into contact with others moving in the same ambit, and (2) deriving and communicating the results of such experience.

This general remark—unexceptionably obvious—is introductory to a chapter in our history, the contents of which would almost certainly have surprised even the most foreseeing of our pious founders half a century ago. We may recall what Miss Shirreff wrote in her pamphlet in 1872: "The National Union" (the parent of our thirty-eight schools) "is still a small body, a poor one, without power, trusting to no assistance from Government, to no influence of Party, yet hoping to do a good work." If Miss Shirreff could revisit us to-day, and accompany us through our progress of the schools enumerated in the last chapter, her keen intelligence would recognize at once that Government, and even Party—for the influence of the Labour Party is very strong, and, when justly inspired, very properly strong, in regulating the flow of public money—are now most significant factors in the good work that we still try to do.

What Miss Shirreff would think of that increase in our Trust's dependence on other bodies, it would be a waste of time to ask. "Whatever is, is right," they said in the eighteenth century, and the councils of the immortals may attain to a super-Augustan peace. Even in our limited vision, it is clear that the development

M

has been inevitable, and that State-aid and even rate-aid for our schools have been the necessary concomitants of the certificates of merit which we have sought for our pupils and teachers. A public school—and we founded public schools—must conform to and satisfy public standards; and the lonely women who set out in 1872 to substitute public day schools for girls for the young ladies' private academies and seminaries, though they might turn away with an Olympian smile from some of the formularies of the Board of Education and some of the phylacteries of the Local Representatives, would not reject the grain with the chaff. If we wanted certain benefits, we had to accept certain conditions, and this, from first to last, has been the process of that development. But let us add, not without justification, that the benefits have been mutual. After all, the Board of Education did not come into existence until 1900, when the Council of the Girls' Public Day School Trust had been doing its work in secondary education for girls in more than a dozen schools in the County of London and in more than a dozen other county areas.

The Trust's secretary, Mr A. Maclean, is the author of a valuable book entitled *The Law Concerning Secondary and Preparatory Schools*[1], and on p. 80 of this compendium will be found a table of dates very useful in the present context. Going back to 1839, we come to the constitution of a Committee of (the Privy) Council on Education, of which Sir James Kay-Shuttleworth, afterwards a member of our Council, was, as we have seen[2], the first secretary. In 1853, passing over some minor adjustments, we reach the constitution of a Science and Art Department, created by uniting the Department of Practical Art at the Board of Trade

---

[1] Jordan and Sons, Ltd, Chancery Lane.   [2] Page 28.

with various Government Science Institutions. This new Department was carried on at Marlborough House under the Board of Trade, and *grants* were made for the first time to Science and Art Schools and Classes. In 1856, this Department was transferred from the Board of Trade to the 1839 Committee of Council, whose establishment became the Education Department, and in the following year the Science and Art Department was moved to South Kensington. (The distance between South Kensington and Whitehall came to be measured in other than spatial terms.) In 1864, the Science and Art Department was incorporated by Royal Charter, and the area of its grants was extended in 1859 and 1872. In 1895, Schools of Science were required to provide a certain amount of literary and other instruction, and in 1897, states Mr Maclean, "the restriction which had hitherto confined the benefit of grants to the industrial sections of the community was removed, and many Grammar Schools proceeded to qualify for grants in respect of their science curriculum." In 1899 came the Board of Education Act, determining the Education Department, including the Science and Art Department, and the present writer may fitly rely on the authority of Sir Philip Magnus for an appreciation of the importance of that Act.

"History," he wrote in 1905[1], "will give credit to those true reformers who have converted our long-endured educational chaos into something approaching a regulated system. The closer association of the two often-opposing authorities, Whitehall and South Kensington, the abolition of that educational anomaly, a separate Department of Science and Art, and the recognition of the true place of science and art teaching in the curricula of all schools; the creation of one central authority

[1] *Educational Aims and Efforts*, p. 217. Longmans.

for elementary and secondary education, and the acknowledge-
ment that technical instruction, though no part of either, is a
matter of State concern, as supplementing both,—these great
changes, which, owing to the simplicity of the Acts of Parliament
by which they were introduced, seem small and unimportant,
will be recorded by future chroniclers as epoch-making incidents
in the history of education in this country. No less important,
too, was the consequent legislation of 1902, creating local
authorities, endowed, subject to State control, with somewhat
similar functions, and with the further power of raising money
from the rates for the purposes of education generally."

It was in the midst of these immense changes between 1839 and 1902 that the Girls' Public Day School
Trust came into being, and it was out of this chaos
that its Council had to hammer a consistent policy for
the government of our schools. The chronicler, who,
as Sir Philip Magnus enjoins, is to record these changes
as epoch-making, may note, too, how wisely that
Council adapted them to the heritage which it was
administering.

The new Board of Education got to work with
commendable speed, and in 1904 its Regulations for
Secondary Schools swept away the old provision by
which the grant had been made substantially dependent
on the science and art taught in the school, and provided
for grants being made in respect of the curriculum as
a whole. Most of our schools since 1898 had been
receiving grants from the Science and Art Department
in South Kensington. Now, after 1904, they began
to earn the new grant, and neither the new grants nor
the old were available for schools "carried on for private
profit." It was in order to avoid this disability that the
reform of our constitution, noted at the end of chapter II,
was adopted by the Council. But we shrank for some
years from the further changes which would have been
involved by our acceptance of the Board's "Higher"

Grant, in lieu of the "Lower" Grant, for which we had thus qualified. This question first came before us on July 10th, 1907, when we decided to discuss with our headmistresses the main conditions attached to the higher scale,—that a majority of the Governing Body of the School should consist of representatives of the Local Authority, and that a percentage (fixed, normally, at 25 per cent.) of the pupils should be scholars from public elementary schools. In the following October, it was unanimously resolved, and the resolution was communicated to the Press,

> That the Board of Education be informed that the Council of the Girls' Public Day School Trust do not propose to apply for the higher grant, as in their opinion the conditions prescribed would interfere with their desire to maintain their Schools as Secondary Schools of the highest grade.

Sir William Bousfield was then Chairman of our Council, and though this decision was modified in 1908 in the sole instance of our Carlisle School[1], it was maintained during his reign. But after his death in 1910, the late Prebendary Northcote, who succeeded him in the Chair, became more and more impressed by the financial (and, to his credit, even more by the social and moral) need of abandoning our former attitude. The Building Fund Appeal of 1912, which is noted in chapter 11, and which Mr Northcote did so much to make successful, was a clear indication to some younger members of our Council that we could not much longer resist the pressure of the Board of

[1] Our Minute reads: "The Board of Education have agreed to waive, in the case of Carlisle, Local Representatives on the Council, thus entitling it to the Higher rate of grant for this year and next; but have declined to do so in the cases of Highbury and Paddington." It will be observed that all three Schools are now either closed or transferred.

Education; and to many of us, despite our conservative tendencies, expressed in the resolution of October, 1907, there was even a certain attractiveness in the prospect of getting our schools, with all their brilliant achievement and stores of tradition and experience, more in touch with the Local Authorities, established by the Acts of 1902 and 1903, whose business it was to prepare County area schemes for the co-ordination of all forms of education. Gradually, then, and more and more confidently, we followed our Chairman's lead into the new era. In certain districts, owing to local conditions, we handed our schools over to the Authority: Carlisle, Dover and Paddington will be recalled in this connection from the record in chapter IV; in two schools, Croydon and Ipswich, we accept the Authority's grants, with all the conditions involved; in the rest, we are in receipt of the State grant on the "Higher" scale (which is likely presently, it is said, to be the only scale), and the consequent closer administrative co-operation with the Local Education Authorities has been carried out with a minimum of friction—a result largely due, as we gratefully acknowledge, to the widespread appreciation of our work in every area affected. Many of the Authorities concerned, in their first appointment of Local Representatives to our Council, have paid us the compliment of selecting existing members of that Council to represent them, with not more than one additional representative, so that, in conducting our business, we change our status but not our personnel. In the instances of more distant schools, where an adjustment of this kind would be impracticable, a division of functions has been arranged, which, while it does not deprive us of a real measure of control, gives the school concerned the great advantage of the close and direct interest of its governors. It may be observed in this connection, as a general statement illustrating the particular circumstances, that the extension of local government throughout the country, and the establishment of local universities, have encouraged and stimulated faculties which were only latent fifty years ago, when our Ladies of the Schools went out, with their sheaf of entry-forms and subscription-forms, to sow the harvest which others have reaped.

Two points of interest arise out of the above considerations: (1) the work of our headmistresses in conference, and (2) the relation of our schools to universities. We mentioned just now how in 1907 we called our headmistresses into a consultation on policy, and here we may record that Miss Jones, of our Notting Hill School, was one of the little group of headmistresses, convoked by Miss Buss in 1874 to a meeting, out of which grew the now numerous and influential body known as the Association of Headmistresses. It has been closely connected with our schools, one or another of which has often provided it with a meeting-place. Nearly all our headmistresses have been members of it, and the following have been among its Presidents:

> 1897–99. Miss Jones (Notting Hill).
> 1905–07. Miss F. Gadesden (Blackheath).
> 1907–09. Mrs Woodhouse (Clapham).
> 1915–17. Miss Escott (Sheffield).
> 1917–19. Miss Oldham (Streatham Hill).

Miss Sheldon (Sydenham), Miss Bell (Sutton) and Miss Haig Brown (Oxford) have been among its Treasurers, and Miss Ruth Young, for many years its Secretary, is an old Oxford High School girl.

As time went on, and membership increased, and

the value of conference was better appreciated, it began to be felt by our own headmistresses that they needed opportunities for conferring with one another apart from the heads of other schools. Accordingly, in November, 1901, thirty-one of our headmistresses, forgathered at Wimbledon, arranged to hold an annual meeting of this kind, which has since been cordially recognized by the Council. It elects a Standing Committee of three members, one of whom retires annually after her successor has been chosen by the three in office, and this Standing Committee is not infrequently consulted by the Education Committee of the Council on matters requiring expert advice between the annual conferences each November. On both sides, the system works well,—on all three sides, indeed, it may be said: the headmistresses benefit by the intercourse—younger with older, less experienced with more experienced; they benefit, again, by the free opportunity of putting their views from time to time before the Council; and a member of the Council may say definitely, that the reciprocal advantage of being able to consult expert advice is immensely appreciated by every member of the Governing Body. The June Conference of the Association, which most of our headmistresses attend, is utilized for a special annual meeting between them and the Council of the Trust.

Next, as to universities. These, as stated above, have played a notable part in developing, in the educational sphere, a local sentiment of practical patriotism, and it has been the Council's aim to secure the presence of a university representative on the local Committee of Governors of each School. From the very first, the Trust has welcomed the university hall-mark of efficiency. As early as December, 1873, in a printed scheme of organization for our Notting Hill School, we find a provision that girls in the highest class should take the Cambridge Senior Local Examination, and those in the second class (the next highest) the Junior. In 1874, the Oxford and Cambridge Schools Examination Board was established, and offered to boys' schools of the highest grade (1) a general examination, and (2) certificates exempting their holders under certain conditions from Responsions and the Previous Examination. In January, 1877, after a correspondence between the Chairman of our Council and the Master of Balliol, girls' schools were added to its operation, and in that year seven of our schools were examined by the Board, and a general rule was adopted for such procedure. Occasional conferences were held at the offices of the Trust between the Secretaries to the Board and the Council's Education Committee, which were very much appreciated by the Council for the opportunity which they afforded of discussing the standard and nature of the examination and the teaching in our schools. In 1885, some of our schools sent in candidates for the Board's Higher Certificate, and this, again, gradually became the rule for girls in the Sixth Form. Meanwhile, in 1877, the Council had sanctioned preparation for the Cambridge Higher Local (originally called the examination for women) at the Nottingham High School; and this examination played a conspicuous part in determining the nature of the higher work at several of our schools and particularly at Croydon.

The non-acceptance by London University of the examinations of other universities constantly increased the practice among our pupils, looking forward to a London degree, of taking the London Matriculation while still at school. That examination, until comparatively recent years, was rigid as to the subjects required, and thus caused difficulties of organization in schools enjoying the greater freedom of choice allowed by the Oxford and Cambridge Board and the "Locals." The London Matriculation passed, however, to the opposite extreme, and thus leapt into favour.

The action of the Board of Education brought about a sweeping change in the schools, when it required that a "First School Examination" should be taken, and by complete Forms, about the age of sixteen, and also that a "Second" Examination should be taken at about the age of eighteen. The multiplicity of examinations, of varying character, which the schools had freely used, presented a difficulty, and in order to standardize them, while permitting all the universities to share in a work bound to increase enormously, the Board of Education held an investigation at every university, and eventually accepted as recognized "First" and "Second," certain examinations of Oxford, Cambridge, London, Bristol, Durham and the Northern Universities, as well as of the Oxford and Cambridge Joint Board. The evil of multiplicity is not altogether eliminated, but that closer contact with the local university, out of which the present paragraph opened, has been distinctly furthered by this innovation.

And what of the results?

The faithful chronicler has in front of him a sheaf, laboriously compiled, yet lit by the love that lightens labour, of university and other successes won by pupils in our schools. In all the conversations and conferences which it has been his privilege to hold with the wise ladies who have assisted him in his task, none have been so frequent or so inconclusive as those which have dealt with the question of how to treat such records. The abiding fear that some names have been omitted, through loss of documents, or lapse of memory, or

the death of the headmistress who might have remembered, or the absence of archives, particularly in
the instance of the closed schools, or any other cause,
has oppressed the compilers throughout. Then there is
the difficulty of just comparison, which can only be
solved by a calculus containing a factor of parental
affection, and allowing for differences of age, and size,
and opportunities, in the schools to be compared. Bare
lists of names would emphasize the very differences
which that method would conceal. Accordingly, and
in discharge of the responsibility which his coadjutors
finally confided to him, the chronicler has preferred,
with Herrick,

> Ribbands to flow confusedly,
> A winning wave, deserving note,
> In the tempestuous petticoat,

to an art too precise in every part. He is informed that
over two thousand degrees have been taken in fourteen
universities,—a formidable total in fifty years, and that
nearly eight hundred scholarships have been gained at
universities in that period, and these figures convey an
impressive effect without being distributed through the
schools. For the rest, there is no alternative between
silence and a catalogue. Who could check the omissions,
or lay down the frontiers of inclusion, or supply the
requisite details for the *Gyasque Thoasque* items, if we
chose to adopt the latter method? How should we
relieve the tedium of our readers, or soothe the rivalry
of our correspondents? And if we break the silence,
where shall we begin or end? What of the war-work
of our schoolgirls,—the work done actually in the
schools by wisely directed "Sister Susies," and the
work done by our Old Girls, so many of whom to-day
wear the riband of the Order of the British Empire,
for deeds of valour under fire, or for duller deeds of

heroic endurance in Base-hospitals or in nursing-homes, and some of whom fell for their country as gallantly as any brother in arms[1]? We know of a doctor of science, who, in the early days of the war, worked day and night at inventing means for the supply of the cut-off drugs from Germany, and who learned her science in our Kensington laboratory. We know a pupil of Clapham, who "beat the Senior Wrangler" at Cambridge. We have the privilege of including on our Council three Old Girls of our schools—Mrs Buckler, C.B.E., Rhoda Countess of Carlisle, and Lady Harmer. The stage, music, literature, and all the Muses have found devotees among past pupils of the Trust: there is no field of action open to women in which our Old Girls have not left footprints, the memory of which will be enduring.

And, adding together these chance impressions, gathered, as we have indicated, from a pile of documents, industriously and faithfully collected, may we not hazard the general conclusion, that the end has justified the means, and that the hopes which guided our founders in 1872 have been not unworthily fulfilled by the generations trained in their foundations? It is not easy, living, as we do, in times distraught by many new experiences, uprooting some ancient landmarks, and reversing some former conventions, to isolate one factor of change, and evaluate it separately. The women's movement, as it is called, of which the legislative recognition was by no means the chief part—"it will be the duty of the new Government," wrote Mr

---

[1] It may be of interest to note that the following awards (in addition to general War Medals) were among the distinctions gained by Old Girls of the Trust Schools for services rendered in connection with the War: D.B.E., 1 (Dame Muriel Talbot; Kensington); D.S.O., 1; M.C., 1; Bar to M.C., 1; Military Medal, 2; Military Star, 1914, 2; Royal Red Cross, 11; C.B.E., 3; O.B.E., 11; M.B.E., 19; Mentioned in Dispatches, 11; and Foreign Decorations, 8.

Lloyd George and Mr Bonar Law to the electors of Great Britain and Ireland in November, 1918, "to remove all existing inequalities of the law as between men and women,"—is itself only a part of a movement greater and more inevitable than human laws can follow or keep pace with: the law may lag behind (as before the war), or go too fast (as some think it has hurried since), but the advance of thought and effort and capacity is steady and unperturbed, and in time its operation is likely to be revealed as wholly beneficial to our country. In that day, the aims of our schools, and the multifarious achievements of their pupils, will be accounted, we believe, among the factors that made the new age.

Turning back to Miss F. Gadesden once more, and to the paper which she read at Cambridge at the Summer Meeting of August, 1900, we find the following passage:

The High Schools and Colleges are sending out their pupils to be trained as Doctors and Nurses, Factory Inspectors, Poor Law Guardians, Sanitary Officers, Teachers, Lecturers, Examiners. Not the least of the peaceful revolutions of the nineteenth century is that which has made English Schools places of real education and training, and which has brought to thousands the conception of what is due from them to their homes and to their country. If the schools of to-morrow are consequently as great an improvement on those of to-day as these are on those of yesterday, I, for one, shall be fully satisfied. I know that our best High Schools are better than any that have gone before, and that their influence on girls and women is for good.

Nearly another quarter of a century has passed. Miss Gadesden has retired, and her "morrow" has descended on us suddenly, as out of a storm in the night. But if we compare this passage with that old one mentioned on another page from the *Quarterly Review* of 1869 ("England is not prepared for either female suffrage or a female Parliament, for women as Poor-law guardians, attendants at vestries, public lecturers, doctors, lawyers," and so forth), we can measure the progress that has been made, and, perhaps, evaluate its results. 1869–1900–1923: is England worse or better, nobler or meaner, purer or fouler, for the experience of two generations, in which the change in the public estimation of women's work has been an inseparable element? If the answer is better, nobler, purer, then our schools have deserved well of the State.

THE JUBILEE

It is fitting to close this record with a brief account of the celebration of our Jubilee on June 1st, 1923.

The main feature of the celebration was a solemn Service of Thanksgiving held in St Paul's Cathedral, by permission of the Dean and Chapter. About nine hundred pupils from the Schools occupied the seats under the dome, while the choir was filled by women and men interested in the work of the Trust. The sermon was preached by Dr Inge, Dean of St Paul's, and the following was one of two special Prayers recited on the occasion:

Almighty God, we do offer unto Thee most high praise and hearty thanks for all Thy wonderful graces and virtues which Thou hast manifested in all holy persons upon earth, who by their lives and labours have shined forth as lights in the several generations of the world, such as were Henrietta Maria Stanley of Alderley, Maria Georgina Grey, Emily Shirreff, and Mary Gurney, whom we remember with honour and commemorate with joy; and for whom, as also for all others Thy happy servants who have departed this life, we praise and magnify Thy holy Name; most humbly desiring that we may still continue in the fellowship of their spirit, following with a glad will and mind their holy examples of service and steadfastness. *Amen.*

After the conclusion of the Service, the Headmistresses, Old Girls and other guests of the Trust were entertained at tea by the Council of the Trust at the Guildhall, and parties of present pupils were similarly entertained, by the similarly kind permission of the respective authorities, at the halls of the Cutlers' and Stationers' Companies.

The following "Impression" of the ceremony in St Paul's Cathedral has been specially written by a friend for this volume:

St Paul's looked much as usual with its curious combination of sympathy and aloofness, like a mother reading quietly among her thronging, busy, contentious, pre-occupied children. But gradually the usual gives place to the unusual. Imperceptibly at first the surroundings change, knots of people gather at the great ascending steps, greeting one another, talking eagerly, with an occasional cry of surprise and warmer greeting, knots of people, many young, some old, but the greatest number in middle life; and all women. The gathering increases; omnibuses and char-a-bancs draw up; a large party of girls arrives two and two, with white dresses and coloured hatbands, and passes round to the transept doors; then another, and another. The city stirs vaguely with interest. "What is this? St Paul's is always having odd doings, but what is this?" *This*, to anyone concerned in it, was a curious exhilaration—the assembling of the G.P.D.S.T. from the ends of England to give thanks—a triumph and a dedication.

*   *   *   *   *

Through a small doorway and up an unexpected little spiral stair lay our way to the choir. So dim was the choir on that grey afternoon that at first one only noticed that it was already more than half filled by vaguely distinguishable forms. The half-hour of recollectedness was welcome and well spent. One after another there entered people whose activity in the cause of education was either famous or perhaps only known and appreciated by a few: past Headmistresses, Members of Council, distinguished members of other bodies, who had come to take their part in a celebration which was recognised as of national importance. Chiefly from this inspiring contact, but still only gradually, was a sense quickened of the significance of that great service—the significance to this and future generations, the significance to women, the significance, at the other end of the scale, to the small bit of work for which each one of us stood. It would be impossible henceforth to feel one's work unrelated to more magnificent ventures. It was even now caught up with all its sordidities and irritations, with its red ink and memoranda, into an august and a living whole. There was not a child there so young or so unimaginative that she would not feel in some incoherent way that it was a fine thing for her particular drop of water to be part of the sea. Thus, before the service had begun, that great congregation was bound together in the community of emotion which expresses itself most fully and fitly in the glorious act of corporate singing. The opening hymn with its majestic alleluias gave us just expression for this exultation.

The second aspect of the Service seemed to emerge after this first moment of rejoicing and to find its beautiful and adequate interpretation later in the special prayers. After its first united act of expression that concourse of people seemed in a sense to fall apart and divide into irrevocable generations. We could rejoice in unison with a great volume of sound, but when it came to remembrance, to the deeper kind of thanksgiving, how varied was our equipment! The revered names could carry no significance to many, the very words conveyed a different meaning. From that point there seemed to enter into the service that wistfulness which, to older people, is so much a part of all school celebrations, which is inevitable wherever experience and inexperience meet in close and affectionate fellowship. It would be wrong to suggest that the service lost by this cleavage, it seemed on the contrary to take on a more poignant significance. If there had been any trace of narrowness in the patriotism it was now lost in a more spiritual harmony. Even the youngest must have felt solemnity and reverence in the splendid words of remembrance, of thanksgiving and dedication. To us older people it brought the feeling of that other world where abasement and exaltation are not contrary but complementary to each other. And who has expressed that more burningly than the great apostle to whom the Cathedral Church of St Paul is dedicated!

INDEX

INDEX 199

Huskisson, Miss Mary, 166
Huxley, Thomas Henry, 21, 31–3
— Leonard, 32

Inge, Dr, Dean of St Paul's, 191
Ingle, Mr and Miss, 122
Ipswich Education Authority, 113, 182
Ipswich High School (G.P.D.S.T.), 52, 112–15, 120, 182
Irving, Mrs H. B. (Dorothea Baird), 94
Ivory, Thomas, 67

Jackson, Sir T. G., 90
James, Miss L., 76
Jarrett, Miss, 129
Jefferies, J. R., 112
— Davis. See Davis, Miss K. Jefferies
Jemmett, Miss, 131, 135
Jenny Lind Hospital, 66
Jersey, Dowager Countess of (1912), 24
Jex-Blake, Miss K., 61
— Miss Sophia, 31
Johnson, Miss F., 65
— Miss Florence, 170
— Rev. H. I., 122
Johnston, Miss F. H., 167
Jones, Hugh. See Hugh Jones
— Miss Constance, 40
— Miss Harriet Morant, 21, 47, 48, 51, 58, 59, 62, 149, 183
Julian, Miss E. M., 65, 142, 143

Kay-Shuttleworth, Sir J., 19, 26–8, 33, 34, 44, 50, 178
Kegan Paul family, the, 75
Kemp, T. R., 95
Kennedy, Miss, 143
Kennett, Miss B., 85, 114
Kensington High School (formerly Chelsea High School) (G.P.D.S.T.), 17, 26, 27, 42, 45, 52, 53, 54–8, 89, 93, 104, 135, 144
Kent Education Authority, 142, 182
Ker, Miss M. S., 65
Kimpster, Miss A., 72
Kimpton, Miss Gwynne, 141, 144

King, Canon, 158
— Edward's High School, Birmingham, 165
King's College School, 131
Kitchener, Miss, 111
Knight, Miss D., 118
Knipe, Miss F. M., 166
Krabbe, Miss Ellen, 121
Krause, Miss Marie, 108

Lang, Dr Cosmo (Archbishop of York), 138
Lansdowne, Lord, 24
Latham, William, 33
Laurence, Miss, 108
Lawrence, Sir Henry, 135
— Lord (1873), 19
Leader, J. D., 105
Leahy, Miss, 48, 63, 64, 91, 174, 175
Leary, Mrs, 80
Leblique, Leopold, 102
Le Brun, John, 66, 67
Lecky, Mrs, 41
Ledger, Miss, 137–9
Lee, Miss A. S., 137
Lees, Miss E. M. L., 144, 167
— Miss E. S. 76
Lefroy, Miss, 61
Lennox, Lord Henry, 19
Leverkus, Miss G., 162
Lewis, Miss A. K., 94, 96
— Miss Mabel E., 133, 137
Lewisham Grammar School, 163
Lichfield, Lord and Lady (1873), 19
Limebeer, Miss, 57
Lind, Jenny, 106
Liverpool Education Authority, 176
— High School (G.P.D.S.T.). See Belvedere School, Liverpool
— (East) High School (G.P.D.S.T.). See East Liverpool High School
Lloyd, Miss E., 68
— George, D., 189
Local Education Authorities, 181, 182. And see Bath, Cumberland, Ipswich, Kent, Surrey and Wimbledon
Lodge, Sir Oliver, 176
London Association of School Mistresses, 4
— Bishop of (1873), 19

For EU product safety concerns, contact us at Calle de José Abascal, 56–1°,
28003 Madrid, Spain or eugpsr@cambridge.org.

www.ingramcontent.com/pod-product-compliance
Ingram Content Group UK Ltd.
Pitfield, Milton Keynes, MK11 3LW, UK
UKHW010335140625
459647UK00010B/615